When All Means All

The Constellation of Learning Approach to Student-Centered Schools

Adam D. Drummond-Konopasek

Danny Drummond-Konopasek

ConnectEDD Publishing

Hanover, Pennsylvania

Copyright © 2026 by Adam D. Drummond-Konopasek & Danny Drummond-Konopasek

All rights reserved. No part of this publication may be reproduced, distributed, or transmitted in any form or by any means, including photocopying, recording, or other electronic or mechanical methods, without the prior written permission of the publisher, except in the case of brief quotations embodied in critical reviews and certain other noncommercial uses permitted by copyright law. For permission requests, contact the publisher at: info@connecteddpublishing.com

This publication is available at discount pricing when purchased in quantity for educational purposes, promotions, or fundraisers. For inquiries and details, contact the publisher at: info@connecteddpublishing.com

Published by ConnectEDD Publishing LLC
Hanover, PA
www.connecteddpublishing.com

Cover Design: Kheila Casas

When All Means All —1st ed. Paperback
ISBN: 979-8-9933701-1-8

Praise for *When All Means All*

When All Means All offers a timely, asset-based framework for educators committed to excellence for all learners. By intentionally centering student groups, not subgroups, the book reframes school improvement around belonging, relationships, and inclusive systems. Built on The Constellation of Learning™, it serves as a practical guide for professional learning, helping educators translate data, reflection, and shared values into coherent action that meets the needs of every student.

> —Dr. Joe Brown | Chief Academic Officer, Fort Wayne Community Schools

This book offers a powerful, cohesive roadmap for school transformation, anchored in compelling narrative and disciplined use of evidence. The stories of Maya, Avery, and Elena reveal how even "successful" schools can fail students whose realities don't show up in aggregate metrics. The Constellation of Learning™ provides a clear architecture for aligning systems around specific student groups and rejecting deficit language starting with "subgroup." The authors skillfully weave in current research and national trend data, making the book feel timely and deeply attuned to the post-pandemic landscape. It will be especially valuable for system and school leaders who are ready to interrogate their own definitions of success and redesign policies, schedules, and instructional practices so that "all means all" becomes more than a slogan.

> —Jack Lynch | CEO, HMH

If you truly want to make a lasting and meaningful impact on your students and community, *When All Means All* is essential reading. As both a former student and friend of Dr. Drummond-Konopasek, I experienced firsthand the transformative power of the principles shared in this book. The mentorship, belief, and student-centered approach the authors advocate for are not just theories, they change lives. Without that kind of support and intentional guidance, many students, like me, may never get the opportunity to realize their full potential. For that, I am incredibly thankful

> —Charles Agnew III | Sales Associate at Mercedes-Benz of South Charlotte, NC

When All Means All is a compelling, student-centered guide for educators ready to move equity from intention to impact. Anchored in the Constellation of Learning framework, the book replaces "one more program" reform with purposeful alignment of instruction, leadership, culture, data, and wellness. As a career principal, I found myself deeply affirmed and challenged. The authors speak to the daily realities of our schools, reminding us that belonging drives achievement and that systems must be designed intentionally to serve the needs of every child. Practical, actionable, and deeply human, this book turns belief into action and impact.

> —Melissa D. Patschke, Ed.D. | President of the Board of Directors for the Center of Educational Improvement; Career Elementary Principal; Adjunct Faculty, Immaculata University & Neumann University

Schools that adopt the PLC philosophy are driven towards one common North Star: it is every school's fundamental responsibility to ensure learning at high levels for ALL students. ALL means every single student, regardless of any label placed on them by the school or society. *When All Means All* is an incredible resource for educators to meet this vision for ALL students. It lays out practical evidence-based ideas for supporting each group of students to give them the much-needed sense of belonging and scaffolding so that ALL students will be successful.

> —Dr. Charles Grable | Superintendent, Pioneer Regional School Corporation

When All Means All pushes you to pause, look honestly at your system, and ask who it's really serving. Adam and Danny DrummondKonopasek offer more than slogans; they give a clear, studentcentered way to connect equity, instruction, leadership, and belonging in everyday practice. The Constellation of Learning is a good reminder that real improvement comes from aligning what already matters, not adding more. It's a grounded, practical read for leaders who want "all means all" to show up in the work, not just the talk.

> —Dr. Marc Cohen | Founder, The Leadership Link

A practical, must-read for anyone who cares about kids. Filled with insightful questions and actionable practices, *When All Means All* is the gift that keeps giving, empowering educators to continuously strive to be exceptional humans.

> —Dr. Linda Lucey | VP Conferences, Model Schools Conference

Rarely does a book pair moral courage with practical leadership tools this effectively. *When All Means All* is essential reading for leaders who refuse to play it safe.

> —Danny Bauer Chief Ruckus Maker at Better Leaders Better Schools

When All Means All reminds us that belonging isn't a slogan—It's a choice we make in how we design our schools. Adam and Danny challenge us to move beyond good intentions and build systems where every student is seen, supported, and stretched. After two decades in education, I know folks need practical strategies, research that they work, and deeply human stories to thrive. This book helps us live what we say we believe: that every student matters and a blueprint to do it every day, in every space.

> —Houston Kraft | Author of *Deep Kindness*

When All Means All is a powerful and timely call for schools to move beyond isolated initiatives and intentionally design systems that serve every student. Through the Constellation of Learning framework, the authors show how belonging, high-quality instruction, aligned leadership, and purposeful use of data work together to drive meaningful outcomes. Well organized, engaging, and practical, this book provides clear guidance for educators committed to ensuring success for every learner—and ensuring "all" is not merely an aspiration but a promise fulfilled.

> —Mark Vianello | Superintendent of Schools, Charlotte County Public Schools

As a professor of Educational Leadership and former superintendent, I am often asked by my students how instructional leaders can move from good intentions about equity to coherent systems that ensure every student feels like they belong and succeed. *When All Means All* provides a clear, practical, and ethically grounded answer. Adam and Daniel Drummond-Konopasek position equity not as an initiative, but as the organizing principle of good leadership, instruction, and culture. Through their Constellation of Learning, they offer a model that honors complexity while demanding action. The book's focus on seven interconnected themes represents the essential elements that help every learner thrive. Within those seven themes, there are forty-four actionable ways that translate belief into daily practice, supported by research, reflection, and authentic school examples. This text equips school leaders to design systems that foster belonging, rigor, and student well-being. *When All Means All* is an essential resource for educators, principals, district leaders, instructional coaches, and superintendents committed to equity-driven improvement that gives every student an opportunity to reach for the stars.

> —Dr. Tracy Caddell | Assistant Clinical Professor, Ball State University

When All Means All by Adam D. Drummond-Konopasek and Danny Drummond-Konopasek is the kind of book that will challenge you in the best way. It pushes educators to move beyond good intentions and really examine whether our systems are designed for every student to thrive. The Constellation of Learning framework is thoughtful and practical, giving leaders clear next steps instead of just big ideas. This is not just a book about equity; it's a guide for turning belief into action in ways that actually impact students.

—Dr. Joya Holmes | Executive Director of Professional Learning, Rock Hill School District 3 of York County

In my work with education leaders, I've seen how often strong intentions fail to translate into systems that consistently serve every student. *When All Means All* brings clarity to that challenge. The Constellation of Learning provides a practical and actionable framework that helps leaders examine how leadership, instruction, and culture shape student experience. More importantly, it gives leaders a clear path forward and challenges them to take responsibility for designing systems where every student is known, supported, and able to thrive.

—Vicky Bush | National Leadership and Sales Consultant to Education Organizations

Dedication

This book is first and always dedicated to our four children. Each of you belongs to one of the student groups explored in these pages. Chase, Carson, Carter, and Benjamin—through you, this work became personal long before it became professional. You remind us daily that time matters, that missed moments carry consequences, and that systems must change now—not later—to serve students with dignity, access, and purpose.

Our fierce advocacy in education is rooted in our love for you. It is rooted in a deep sense of justice that demands your educational experiences be both accessible and rigorous, and that you are afforded every opportunity needed to thrive—not someday, but now and into the future. You inspire us to push harder, speak louder, and do better for educators, leaders, and schools so that every child can have the strongest possible outcome.

To Chase, Carson, Carter, and Benjamin: We love you—to infinity and beyond.

Table of Contents

Foreword

The human body must be aligned for movement, balance, and health. Our compasses and maps only guide us when they are calibrated to true north. Satellites must be precisely aligned for GPS systems to determine our position and recalculate our route. Bridges depend on the alignment of load, tension, and structure— misalignment leads to stress, fatigue, and eventual failure. An orchestra requires the alignment of tempo, pitch, timing, and role; when it happens, noise becomes harmony. The constellation of stars must be aligned to become a map, so no one travels in the dark. Teams succeed when purpose, roles, trust, and effort align; talent alone is never enough. Organizations thrive when vision, resources, structures, and incentives point in the same direction. Alignment is how complex systems move from effort to effectiveness— from activity to impact.

So let's review one school. It was doing everything right. Great people. Good intentions. Lots of initiatives. If you walked the halls, you'd see bright spots everywhere. A classroom full of belonging; another full of rigor; another using data well; and another leading innovation. But students told a different story. Some felt known. Others invisible. Some knew what success looked like. Others guessed. Some learned from mistakes. Others learned to hide them. The problem wasn't a lack of stars. The problem was that they weren't aligned.

What was needed, and a major theme of this book, is to stop asking, "What should we add next?" and start asking, "What must line up so learning works for every student?"

What is needed is an alignment of clarity (so everyone knew what success looked like), an alignment of belonging (so no student had to earn the right to be seen), an alignment of teaching (so high-impact practices reached every classroom), an alignment of interpreting data (so it explained what was happening to students, not what was wrong with them), and an alignment of leadership—so it built trust, not compliance. This constellation of factors needs to occur for teachers, students–for all–and it happens not when we add more stars, but when we align the ones we already have.

So many leaders add programs, develop initiatives, and create missions. The Drummond-Konopasek team argues that such program-centered reform needs to be replaced with student-centered design. This book introduces *The Constellation of Learning* as a coherent framework for building schools in which every student—across identity, ability, language, and circumstance—experiences belonging, access, and accelerated learning. It starts with the premise that schools are intrinsically moral, relational, and instructional systems that must be intentionally designed around every student's improvement. It rejects deficit language and compliance-driven reform. Rather than offering another list of initiatives, the book provides a navigational model: seven interdependent themes (the "stars" of the constellation) that must align if improvement is to be sustained. The argument is clear: when any star dims, learning suffers; when they align, improvement becomes possible for all.

The model is built around seven major claims: "All means all" is a design problem, not a belief problem; student groups must be centered, not remediated; belonging is a prerequisite for learning, not a byproduct; instructional coherence matters more than isolated excellence; leadership is adaptive, distributed, and relational; data must humanize, not label; and well-being is structural, not supplemental. Where Paul Simon famously catalogued *50 Ways to Leave Your Lover*, Adam and Danny give us *44 Ways to enable schools to have high impact*—by turning our beliefs about students into actions that actually improve schools. The "Ways" are a standout feature: practical, immediately usable strategies that connect belief to daily decision-making. They prevent the book from remaining aspirational and anchor it in instructional and leadership moves.

If a leader asks, "Which practices should we invest in?" then read *Visible Learning*. If a leader asks: "Why do our most vulnerable students still miss out on those practices—and what must we redesign?" then read this book. Schools need to work not just for *some* students, but for *all* students. The stars must be aligned.

John Hattie
Melbourne Laureate Professor Emeritus

Introduction

I'll never forget Maya, Avery, and Elena.

One Saturday morning in February, I was in my office working—like I often did—on long-term planning and strategy. The building was quiet, the halls empty. I was deep into reviewing NWEA MAP data, scanning achievement and growth trends, when my office phone rang.

I remember being surprised. Calls rarely came in on Saturdays, and I assumed it was a voicemail waiting to be left.

I answered the phone anyway.

It was Kim—the mother of twin fifth graders, Maya and Avery, and their younger sister, Elena, a third grader. From the moment she began speaking, it was clear she wasn't calling to ask a question or seek clarification. She was calling because she was angry. And hurt.

Her words came fast and sharp. She described incident after incident—her daughters being bullied for being Black, feeling unsafe, feeling unseen. She shared her fear that they were falling behind academically and her belief that the school was doing nothing to stop it.

I tried to interject. I tried to explain. I tried to defend the work we were doing.

And then I realized something important.

I needed to stop talking.

So I listened. I let Kim share every example, every concern, every moment she had been carrying—one after another. It was a long list. And by the time she finished, one truth was unmistakable:

She believed we had failed each of her daughters.

It didn't matter what supports we had in place. It didn't matter what data I could reference or programs I could name. I could have responded with my own list—interventions, meetings, strategies—but none of it would have changed what she felt.

Her experience told her we had failed. And in that moment, that experience mattered more than my intentions.

So instead of defending, I asked one question:

"How can we work together to change this story?"

Maya, Avery, and Elena represent multiple student groups that appear throughout this book—Black students, students experiencing poverty, students who have faced housing instability, and students with disabilities. Elena, in particular, was navigating school with a diagnosed disability, adding another layer to her experience.

That phone call marked a turning point in my career. I had believed our school was successful. The data suggested we were. But I learned that day that success defined only by achievement and growth can hide important truths. Because perception is reality—and for this family, the reality was that we had not done enough.

Throughout this book, you will return to Maya, Avery, and Elena. Their story—and stories like theirs—will resurface as we examine student groups who are too often overlooked, misunderstood, or unintentionally left behind.

Our hope is that these stories resonate with you, challenge your assumptions, and push your thinking beyond what feels comfortable. Because when we are willing to confront the stories we'd rather not hear, we create the possibility for real change

Illuminating The Constellation of Learning™

Teaching is the only profession in the world that impacts three generations of families at the same time: students, their parents/guardians, and their future children. If students have a positive educational experience, they will be more likely to raise children who have a more positive perspective on school. However, if students have a negative experience, they may likely raise children that do not appreciate or value education. As educators, we are truly privileged to have this type of impact in our community.

Education is the one system that touches every child, every family, and every community. Yet, in schools across the nation, too many students still walk through the doors each morning unseen, misunderstood, or lost. They are intelligent, curious, and capable—but the structures around them are often designed for someone else. *When All Means All* was born from this tension: the widening gap between what we know about how student groups learn and what too many still experience.

We wrote this book because the promise of *all means all* has yet to be fully realized. Even as educators commit themselves to every learner's success, systemic barriers persist. National Assessment of Educational Progress (NAEP) data show that reading and math scores for nine-year-olds dropped to their lowest levels in more than two decades after the pandemic (NCES, 2024). Chronic absenteeism has doubled in many districts (Balfanz & Byrnes, 2023). According to the National Center for Education Statistics, special education teacher vacancies are at record highs, while multilingual learner enrollment continues to rise. These realities remind us that improvement cannot be achieved through programs alone—it depends on people who act as *change agents* for students.

The Constellation of Learning:
Guiding Pathways to Educational Excellence.

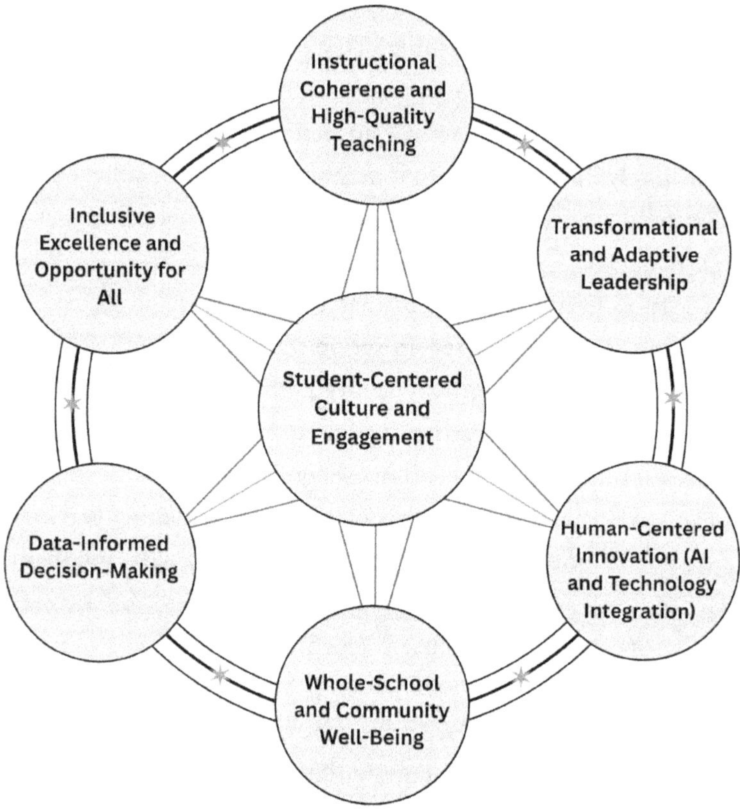

To guide that work, we built this book around a leadership model we call **The Constellation of Learning™: Guiding Pathways to Educational Excellence.** Like stars forming a pattern in the night sky, the seven interconnected themes represent the essential elements that help every learner thrive. Each theme offers a different vantage point, but together they create a navigational map—illuminating a clear, student-centered path forward.

Theme 1: Inclusive Excellence and Opportunity for All

Inclusive excellence begins with a belief—that brilliance exists in every classroom and that equity is not a program but a daily practice. It means confronting the opportunity gaps that still separate who has access from who is merely present. Despite years of reform, the 2023 *Condition of Education* report from the National Center for Education Statistics found that students from historically marginalized backgrounds are still less likely to be enrolled in advanced coursework, even when they meet proficiency benchmarks.

> Creating inclusive excellence requires leaders who see equity as excellence, not charity.

Creating inclusive excellence requires leaders who see equity as excellence, not charity. It is a call to examine grading systems, access to rigorous curriculum, and the subtle signals that communicate belonging. Within this constellation, inclusion is the gravitational pull that keeps every other theme aligned. It asks educators to design environments in which every student—regardless of race, language, income, ability, or identity—feels known and valued.

Theme 2: Instructional Coherence and High-Quality Teaching

Instructional coherence ensures that students experience learning as connected, purposeful, and aligned across classrooms. When instruction is fragmented, students—particularly those who need stability the most—bear the weight of inconsistency. Research from TNTP's *Opportunity Myth* (2023 update) revealed that fewer than one-third of U.S. classrooms provide students grade-level assignments with meaningful feedback.

High-quality teaching has greater impact when educators implement high-effect size strategies with shared clarity and coherence across the school. It blends evidence-based instructional practices with clarity about what success looks like for all learners. Whether through universal design for learning, explicit vocabulary instruction, or culturally responsive pedagogy, coherent systems transform isolated acts of teaching into collective efficacy.

This theme anchors the reflective tools in this book because planning, feedback, and collaboration are where consistency turns into impact.

Theme 3: Transformational and Adaptive Leadership

Leadership in education is no longer about managing change—it is about creating the conditions allowing change to occur. Transformational leaders articulate vision and align people around shared purpose. Adaptive leaders recognize that the challenges before us—unfinished learning, staff burnout, and the politicization of schooling—are not technical problems with quick fixes, but adaptive ones that require learning, experimentation, and courage.

High-quality teaching multiplies its impact when educators, leading through influence rather than title, implement high-effect size strategies with shared clarity and coherence across a school. When instructional decisions are aligned and consistently enacted, individual expertise becomes collective efficacy, strengthening outcomes for both students and staff.

Recent RAND (2024) data show that principal turnover now exceeds eighteen percent nationally, the highest rate in more than a decade. Leadership stability and adaptability are directly correlated with teacher retention and student outcomes. Within this constellation, transformational and adaptive leadership form the engine that sustains improvement. They remind us that influence is distributed, not positional—and that every teacher can lead change from where they stand.

Theme 4: Human-Centered Innovation (AI and Technology Integration)
We are living through a technological inflection point. Artificial intelligence, digital learning ecosystems, and adaptive assessment tools are reshaping what it means to teach and learn. Yet technology's value depends entirely on how human we allow it to remain. Human-centered innovation invites us to leverage emerging tools without losing empathy, creativity, or connection.

According to the 2024 ED Week Research Center survey, 67 percent of teachers report using generative AI tools for lesson planning, but fewer than half feel confident that their districts provide guidance for ethical use. The opportunity is clear: when innovation centers on students' humanity, technology amplifies—not replaces—the teacher's role.

Throughout this book, stories and strategies illustrate how schools thoughtfully use digital tools to personalize learning, remove barriers for students with disabilities, and support multilingual access. Human-centered innovation ensures that progress remains grounded in purpose.

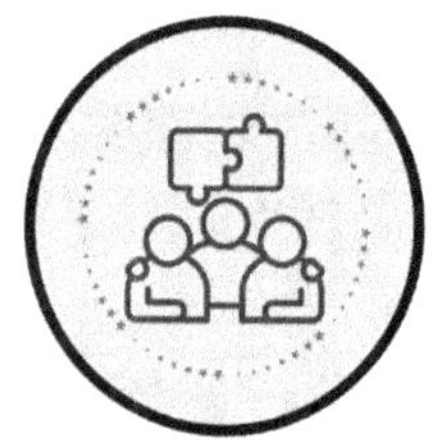

Theme 5: Student-Centered Culture and Engagement

At the heart of the constellation lies the student. Culture and engagement define whether students feel that school is *for* them. The University of Chicago's 5Essentials Framework reminds us that a supportive environment and ambitious instruction are two of the five strongest predictors of an organized school that yield achievement results for students. Yet Gallup's 2024 State of Education report found that only forty-six percent of students feel engaged most of the day at school.

A student-centered culture is not accidental; it is built through relationships, relevance, and rigor. This theme threads through every element in the book because engagement is both a cause and a consequence of equity. When students see themselves reflected in the curriculum, trust their teachers, and understand the purpose behind learning, they do more than participate—they belong.

Theme 6: Data-Informed Decision-Making

Numbers tell stories—but only when we listen. Data-informed decision-making transforms information into insight and action. Schools strong in at least three of the 5Essentials are ten times more likely to improve student outcomes (UChicago Consortium, 2020). Yet data use remains inconsistent across districts. Frankly, we are data inundated and overwhelmed on where to start.

This theme calls for balance: data as a mirror, not a hammer. Educators in this book learn to disaggregate results by student group, analyze patterns in attendance, course enrollment, or discipline, and ask not, "What is wrong with these students?" but, "What is happening to these students?" When data drives empathy and improvement rather than judgment, every learner benefits.

Theme 7: Whole-School and Community Well-Being

No student thrives in isolation. Learning is deeply connected to physical safety, emotional regulation, and a sense of belonging within a broader community. After the pandemic, the CDC's 2024 Youth Risk Behavior Survey found that nearly thirty percent of high school students reported persistent feelings of sadness or hopelessness—an alarming reminder that well-being is foundational, not peripheral, to learning.

Whole-school well-being involves caring for both students and adults. It asks schools to design systems where psychological safety, collaboration, and restorative practices are as valued as test scores. It recognizes that families, community agencies, and partners are integral parts of the learning ecosystem. In this constellation, well-being is the connective tissue that sustains every other theme.

Connecting the Stars: Why We Wrote This Book

Each of these seven themes reflects a principle we have seen come to life in our own classrooms, coaching conversations, and leadership journeys. When any single star in the constellation dims, learning suffers. But when they shine together, schools become places where every student can soar. This belief is not theoretical for us—it is rooted in lived experience, shaped by hard-earned lessons, and strengthened by moments of transformation we have witnessed alongside educators across the country.

We also know that progress is personal. Improvement rarely begins in a policy; it begins in a classroom—through one teacher's decision to re-examine grading bias, one counselor's commitment to check in on a student experiencing homelessness, one principal's willingness to redesign schedules to ensure inclusion. These moments matter because they reveal what is possible. This book was written to help educators move from moments of insight to systems of support that last—beyond individual classrooms, beyond a single school year.

Schools and districts committed to meaningful improvement must be willing to examine both performance and growth through the lens of student groups. Aggregate data can surface trends, but it often obscures the lived realities of learners whose experiences with schooling are shaped by access, identity, language, disability, or circumstance. When educators intentionally review how different student groups are performing and growing—and ask *why* those patterns exist—they begin to see beyond outcomes to the conditions producing them.

Understanding the challenges underperforming student groups face allows schools to move from generic solutions to targeted, responsive action. Instructional strategies, support structures, and leadership decisions become more powerful when they are aligned to real barriers rather than assumptions. In this way, equity work shifts from intention to impact. By responding to student group needs with clarity and care, schools design systems in which improvement is purposeful—and where success is not reserved for some students, but possible for every learner.

Student Groups are the Core of the School

Throughout this book, we intentionally and unapologetically use the term *student group* rather than *subgroup*. This is not a stylistic choice—it is a values stance. The word *sub* literally means less than, secondary, or beneath, and language that diminishes students has no place in a profession committed to equity and belonging. The student groups named in this book are not on the margins of our work; they are its core. Just as a star draws its energy and light from its center, schools draw their purpose and power from the students they serve. If we are serious about ensuring every child gets what every child needs, our language must reflect that commitment.

This matters because words do not live only on pages—they live in policies, accountability systems, data dashboards, and improvement plans. When student groups are labeled as *sub*, they are too easily treated as secondary in decision-making, resourcing, and urgency. Too often, systems analyze these students after the fact, address them as exceptions, or reduce them to compliance checkboxes rather than centering their experiences in improvement work. By rejecting deficit language, we challenge schools and districts to redesign how they collect data, set goals, allocate support, and measure success. Centering student groups means beginning improvement with those who have been historically underserved—not as an add-on, but as the starting point for equity-driven action.

For that reason, we will not use the word *subgroup* anywhere in this book. We invite educators to make the same intentional shift—because the work begins with what we choose to name.

Eleven Chapters, Forty-Four Ways, Additional Resources

The body of this book is organized into eleven chapters, each spotlighting a distinct student group whose experiences illuminate the broader constellation of learning:

1. **Students in Poverty** explores the intersection of socio-economic adversity and academic opportunity, offering practical ways to remove barriers and elevate hope.

2. **Students with Disabilities** reframes special education through a strengths-based lens, emphasizing access, collaboration, and inclusive design.

3. **Students Experiencing Homelessness** centers the power of stability, dignity, and belonging for learners navigating housing insecurity.

4. **Black Students** celebrates excellence, confronts systemic bias, and offers actionable paths to culturally sustaining pedagogy.

5. **Students from Undocumented Homes** examines fear, resilience, and advocacy within families seeking safety and opportunity.

6. **Hispanic Students** explores linguistic richness, identity affirmation, and family partnership as pathways to achievement.

7. **Native American Students** honors sovereignty, heritage, and storytelling while addressing the persistent invisibility of Indigenous learners.

8. **English Learners (EL)** bridges language, culture, and content to transform multilingualism into an asset for the entire school community.

9. **High-Ability Students** expands the conversation on equity by ensuring gifted learners are challenged, not overlooked.

10. **LGBTQIA+ Students** champions authenticity and safety through inclusive practices that validate every student's identity.

11. **The General Education Student: The Invisible Student** concludes by focusing on the often-overlooked "average" learner, exploring how universal design benefits everyone.

Across these chapters are forty-four actionable "Ways"—intentional practices, strategies, and frameworks educators can implement immediately. Each Way translates belief into action, anchoring student-centered values in daily instructional and leadership decisions. Grounded in one or more themes within the constellation, the "Ways" move schools beyond good intentions toward coherent, sustained practice. Together, they form a roadmap for building schools where *all means all* is not a slogan but a system.

Each chapter in *When All Means All* follows a consistent structure designed to move readers from understanding to action. Embedded throughout the chapters are recurring elements that elevate different voices, bridge systems and practice, and support educators in translating insight into meaningful change. Included within each chapter we mention several resources. These resources are here to help you navigate and carry out the important work of helping all students be successful. The full list of these resources is listed at the end of the book and can be found at our website: **www.WhenAllMeansAll.com** We encourage you to print them and use them frequently. Additionally, you will find some examples of these resources sprinkled throughout the book.

Finally, all chapters end with two features:

- **Hallway Confessions – Daily Practice & Perspective**
  This feature captures the realities of daily practice, surfacing the lived experiences, tensions, and reflections educators encounter in real classrooms and schools. It grounds the work in authenticity, reminding readers that change happens in human moments, not abstractions.
- **The Dismissal Bell – The Five A's**
  Each chapter concludes with a call to action organized around the Five A's—Audit, Adjust, Advocate, Assemble, and Attitude Ask—guiding educators to reflect, plan, and move forward with purpose. This closing ensures that learning does not end with reflection, but with responsibility.

How The Constellation of Learning™ Themes Intersect with Each Chapter

Every chapter is a microcosm of the constellation, shining a different light on the shared mission of student-centered change.

- **Inclusive Excellence and Opportunity for All** threads through every chapter, but it is especially central in Chapters 1, 5, 6, and 8, where systemic access and belonging drive the narrative.
- **Instructional Coherence and High-Quality Teaching** anchors Chapters 2, 9, and 10, where evidence-based practice and aligned instruction directly influence outcomes for students with disabilities, high-ability learners, and multilingual learners.
- **Transformational and Adaptive Leadership** underpins Chapters 3 and 4, emphasizing the courageous leadership required to dismantle barriers for students experiencing homelessness and those from undocumented homes.
- **Human-Centered Innovation** surfaces in Chapters 2 and 10, highlighting how technology can create access for students with disabilities and multilingual learners when guided by empathy.
- **Student-Centered Culture and Engagement** pulses throughout Chapters 5, 6, 7, and 8, where identity, representation, and cultural connection foster engagement.
- **Data-Informed Decision-Making** is embedded across all chapters but most explicitly in Chapter 1 and Chapter 11, guiding reflection on how data illuminate hidden patterns of inequity.
- **Whole-School and Community Well-Being** is most visible in Chapters 3, 4, 7, and 11, where stability, trust, partnerships, and collective responsibility are essential to student success. These chapters highlight that learning does not occur in isolation and that sustainable improvement depends on coordinated care across classrooms, families, and communities.

Constellation Learning Themes by Chapter - A Visual Representation		
Constellation Theme	**Chapters Where the Theme Is Most Prominent**	**How the Theme Shapes the Narrative**
Inclusive Excellence and Opportunity for All	Chapters 1, 5, 6, and 8	Centers systemic access and belonging, emphasizing structures and expectations that ensure dignity, inclusion, and opportunity for every learner.
Instructional Coherence and High-Quality Teaching	Chapters 2, 9, and 10	Highlights evidence-based practice and aligned instruction that improve outcomes for students with disabilities, high-ability learners, and multilingual learners.
Transformational and Adaptive Leadership	Chapters 3 and 4	Emphasizes courageous leadership that dismantles barriers for students experiencing homelessness and those from undocumented homes.
Human-Centered Innovation	Chapters 2 and 10	Explores technology as a tool for access and equity when guided by empathy and human-centered design.

Constellation Learning Themes by Chapter - A Visual Representation		
Constellation Theme	Chapters Where the Theme Is Most Prominent	How the Theme Shapes the Narrative
Student-Centered Culture and Engagement	Chapters 5, 6, 7, and 8	Reinforces identity, representation, and cultural connection as drivers of engagement and learning.
Data-Informed Decision-Making	All chapters; most explicit in Chapters 1 and 11	Uses data to surface inequities, guide reflection, and inform instructional and leadership decisions.
Whole-School and Community Well-Being	Chapters 3, 4, 7, and 11	Highlights stability, trust, partnerships, and collective responsibility across schools, families, and communities.

When read together, the eleven chapters form a continuous story—a movement from understanding individual student experiences to constructing the systems that sustain them. The constellation metaphor becomes more than imagery; it is the architecture of hope.

Where to Start

Reaching ambitious school goals begins with an honest examination of student group performance and growth. Before initiatives are launched or strategies selected, educators must first understand which student groups are thriving, which are underperforming, and where opportunity gaps persist. Systemic data analysis—disaggregated by student group—creates a shared starting point for improvement. When schools ground their work in evidence rather than assumption, next steps become intentional, aligned, and far more likely to produce meaningful change.

> When schools ground their work in evidence rather than assumption, next steps become intentional, aligned, and far more likely to produce meaningful change.

This book is designed to serve as an entry point once those patterns are visible. By pairing data-informed insight with practical strategies, *When All Means All* helps educators move from identifying need to responding with purpose. Rather than relying on one-size-fits-all solutions, leaders and teachers can use the chapters to determine how best to support the specific student groups reflected in their data. In doing so, schools shift from reactive efforts to strategic action—ensuring that improvement plans are not only well intentioned, but well designed.

Consider the use of a Data Teams process that provides a disciplined, collaborative structure for turning data into action. Teams begin by collectively examining student performance and growth data, disaggregated by student group, to identify priority needs. Once a focus area is established, educators analyze patterns and root causes, asking what instructional, systemic, or environmental factors may be contributing to the results. Teams then select and implement targeted strategies, monitor progress through short-cycle formative data, and adjust instruction and support based on evidence of impact. This continuous cycle ensures that data use remains human-centered, responsive, and focused on improving outcomes for every learner.

A Call to Action

We stand at a defining moment for education. The last few years have stretched teachers, leaders, and students to their limits, exposing inequities we can no longer explain away or postpone. What we choose to do next matters—because when educators lead with empathy, act on evidence, and move together with resolve, schools can either remain unchanged or become catalysts for justice and possibility. This book is a call to action for those who refuse to wait, who believe every learner deserves more than survival, and who are ready to lead with urgency toward lasting change.

> What we choose to do next matters—because when educators lead with empathy, act on evidence, and move together with resolve, schools can either remain unchanged or become catalysts for justice and possibility.

When All Means All challenges us to look up and connect the stars—to recognize how each theme, each chapter, and each student is part of a larger, unfinished promise. Our collective responsibility is not simply to admire brilliance, but to remove the barriers that keep it constrained by circumstance. This work demands more than reflection; it calls for decisive action, sustained commitment, and the courage to redesign systems that no longer serve all learners. Together, we can build schools that do more than include every student—we can create places where every learner's light is seen, protected, and allowed to shine.

CHAPTER 1

Students in Poverty: Breaking Cycles, Building Pathways to Opportunity

Opening Vignette

Morning light filtered through the cracked blinds of the small apartment as Jordan pulled on a worn hoodie and waited for the sound of the school bus. His mom had already left for her second job. The fridge hummed, mostly empty except for a carton of milk and an opened jar of peanut butter. Jordan's homework—half done—sat beside a stack of unopened bills. Still, he looked at his younger sister asleep on the couch and whispered to himself, "I've got this."

When Jordan arrived at school, he moved quickly down the hallway, hood up, trying not to draw attention. What his teachers didn't see were the invisible weights he carried: hunger, worry, and the pressure to be the stable one at home. In math class, his eyes darted between the clock and the free breakfast menu taped to the wall. When the bell rang, he smiled faintly at his teacher's "good morning" and hurried to the cafeteria.

Jordan is one of the millions of students in the United States who come to school carrying more than a backpack. Each day, students like him face barriers that shape their confidence, attention, and hope. But Jordan's story isn't one of tragedy—it's one of possibility. When adults look beyond circumstance and see potential, poverty stops being an identity and becomes a context we can respond to with empathy, strategy, and purpose.

Framing the Challenge

According to the U.S. Census Bureau (2023), nearly one in six children in the United States live in poverty. That's roughly 11.6 million students, many of whom arrive at school facing food insecurity, unstable housing, and inconsistent access to health care and internet connectivity. The National Center for Education Statistics (2024) reports that schools with higher concentrations of poverty continue to experience lower achievement growth, chronic absenteeism, and higher staff turnover rates.

Poverty is not a lack of ability—it is a lack of access. The stress of scarcity affects working memory, problem-solving, and emotional regulation. Research from the American Psychological Association (APA, 2023) found that children experiencing chronic financial insecurity show elevated cortisol levels, which can limit concentration and motivation.

But here's the truth: poverty does not predetermine a student's trajectory. When we center relationships, strengthen systems of support, and ensure access to enrichment opportunities, students in poverty can and do thrive. The question for us becomes, "How can we transform school into a place of abundance, where every child's potential is amplified rather than diminished by circumstance?"

The following four "Ways" illustrate how educators and leaders can translate empathy into action—ensuring that students experiencing poverty are met with opportunity, not pity.

Too often, excellence is treated as a fixed trait—something students either possess or lack—rather than a responsibility systems must cultivate. When schools redefine excellence as belonging, access, and invitation, different outcomes become possible. Excellence is not reserved for the privileged; it's revealed when every student feels seen, valued, and invited to rise.

> Excellence is not reserved for the privileged; it's revealed when every student feels seen, valued, and invited to rise.

Way 1 — Reframing the Narrative: Seeing Students, Not Situations

What?

This Way invites us to slow down and examine the stories we tell—out loud and internally—about students in poverty. Too often, those stories focus on what families lack rather than what students bring with them: resilience, adaptability, creativity, and strong relational instincts. Language matters because it shapes expectations long before instruction ever begins. The words educators use in meetings, classrooms, and casual conversations quietly signal who is believed in and what is considered possible.

Reframing the narrative does not deny the very real challenges associated with poverty. Instead, it rejects the assumption that circumstance defines capacity. This Way centers on shifting from deficit-based language that explains away outcomes to asset-based language that reinforces dignity, belief, and responsibility. When educators learn to see students first—not situations—school culture begins to move from sympathy to agency and from explanation to action.

Why?

Research has long affirmed that expectations influence outcomes. Rosenthal and Jacobson's work on the Pygmalion Effect demonstrates that students tend to rise or fall in response to the beliefs held about them by the adults in their lives (Rosenthal & Jacobson, 2018). When educators communicate belief—explicitly and implicitly—students are more likely to persist, engage, and perform. When expectations soften, opportunity often follows suit.

For students in poverty, deficit-based narratives can quietly justify lowered academic press, reduced access to enrichment, or fewer opportunities to demonstrate brilliance. Over time, these patterns compound, shaping both student identity and adult decision-making. Asset-based language disrupts this cycle by reinforcing a critical truth: economic circumstance does not determine potential. Reframing the narrative is foundational work. Without it, even well-intended instructional strategies risk being undermined by unexamined assumptions and diminished belief.

How?

Reframing the narrative begins with awareness and grows through consistent modeling and shared practice. This work is not about perfection or policing language—it is about aligning beliefs, words, and actions around what students deserve and what educators control.

1. Audit everyday language for deficit framing
Listen closely to how students are described in meetings, hallways, and documentation. Replace labels such as "at-risk" with language

that centers potential, and eliminate shorthand phrases that reduce students to circumstances rather than learners.

2. Align shared language with stated values

Ensure that the language used in policies, communications, and professional conversations reflects the school's commitment to growth and access. As discussed in the introduction, intentionally using "student groups" reinforces equity and shared belonging.

3. Elevate perseverance alongside achievement

Create visible opportunities to recognize effort, persistence, and problem-solving through announcements, bulletin boards, or classroom routines. Celebrating how students learn communicates belief in the process, not just the outcome.

4. Model dignity through person-first language

Use language that affirms humanity and respect, such as "students experiencing poverty," rather than labels that define students by circumstance. Consistent modeling sets expectations and normalizes respectful language across the community.

Reflection Prompts

- How does the language we use reveal our expectations of students in poverty?
- Where might deficit-based narratives be quietly influencing instructional or placement decisions?
- Whose strengths and perseverance are currently under-recognized in our school culture?

Then What?

When schools intentionally reframe the narrative, cultural shifts become visible. Conversations about students sound different. Educators speak with greater care and clarity, and recognition extends beyond grades to include growth, persistence, and effort.

Students experience classrooms where belief is explicit and dignity is reinforced through daily interactions.

Over time, shared language becomes part of the school's identity rather than an individual choice. Developing a common language of belief strengthens coherence across classrooms and teams. Schools can deepen this work by tracking how barriers are identified and addressed, reinforcing the belief that challenges are solvable rather than defining. To help teams surface recurring access challenges, **Resource 1.1: Barrier Mapping Template** (*Visit www. WhenAllMeansAll.com to access all resources*) provides a structured way to identify barriers that quietly interfere with learning.

What If?

What if colleagues see this work as semantics or resist changing familiar language? Resistance often reflects habit rather than disagreement. Language shifts can feel uncomfortable before they feel natural. Begin by modeling asset-based language consistently in your own practice. Invite a colleague to join you in being intentional during meetings or classroom conversations. As the language becomes normalized and its impact becomes visible, others are more likely to engage, allowing momentum to grow through example rather than mandate.

Way 2 — Building a Culture of Belonging: Connection Before Correction

What?

Students experiencing poverty often move through school feeling watched more than known. This Way names belonging as a daily practice, not a personality trait or a climate slogan. It asks adults to lead with connection before correction so students experience school as a place where they are invited, recognized, and valued before they are evaluated.

John Hattie's *Visible Learning* research (2024) identifies belonging as a high-impact influence on learning, with an effect size of 0.46—more than a year's worth of academic growth when students feel they belong at school. When students feel invited, known, accepted, involved, supported, befriended, and cared for, engagement rises even when circumstances outside of school remain unchanged. This Way is not about lowering expectations or excusing behavior. It is about creating the conditions where students are willing to engage with learning because they trust the people asking them to do the hard work.

Why?

Students living in poverty often arrive at school already carrying stress—worry about food, housing, family responsibilities, or safety. When classrooms lead with correction, those stressors intensify. Students quickly learn whether school is a place that sees them as a problem to manage or a person worth knowing.

Hattie's research also identifies teacher–student relationships as one of the most powerful influences on achievement, with an effect size of 0.62—again, more than a year's worth of growth. Strong relationships do not remove challenges, but they buffer stress and increase motivation. Students are more willing to take academic risks, persist through difficulty, and recover from mistakes when they believe the adults in the room are for them.

As schools work to elevate student voice and strengthen relationships, **Resource 1.2: Belonging Board Guide** offers a visible, collective approach for increasing awareness of who feels seen and valued. Without intentional structures, belonging becomes uneven. Some students receive frequent affirmation, while others—often students experiencing poverty—remain invisible until something goes wrong. Over time, that imbalance shows up as disengagement, discipline, and missed opportunities to learn.

How?

Belonging is built through intentional adult actions repeated consistently over time. These steps focus on what educators do every day to ensure connection comes before correction.

1. Commit to 2×10 Connections

Spend two minutes a day for ten consecutive school days intentionally connecting with a student who appears disengaged or frequently corrected. Keep the focus on listening, noticing, and learning about the student as a person rather than discussing academics or behavior. Consistency is what signals care and builds trust.

2. Make Identity Visible in the Learning Space

Ensure every student can see themselves reflected through displayed work, interests, cultural references, or community stories. Avoid limiting visibility to high-performing students or polished products. When identity is visible, students receive a daily message that they belong without having to earn it.

3. Build Choice into Learning Design

Offer structured choices in how students access content or demonstrate learning, such as project formats, reading options, or discussion roles. Align choices to learning goals so rigor remains intact. Choice communicates respect and increases ownership simultaneously.

4. Name Strengths Before Addressing Struggles

Intentionally recognize effort, persistence, collaboration, and growth before redirecting behavior or correcting errors. This practice reframes feedback within a relationship rather than a power struggle. Over time, students associate school with growth instead of constant correction.

Reflection Prompts

- Which students receive the most corrective feedback, and which receive the most connection?
- Whose identities and experiences are currently visible in our classrooms and common spaces?
- How often do we name strengths before addressing mistakes?
- Where might our routines unintentionally prioritize control over belonging?

Then What?

In the short term, classrooms begin to feel different. Students participate more readily, take academic risks, and recover more quickly from setbacks. Teachers notice fewer power struggles and more productive conversations, particularly with students who previously seemed withdrawn or resistant. Early indicators appear in attendance, engagement, and the tone of daily interactions.

Over time, the impact extends beyond individual classrooms. Teams develop a shared language around belonging, supported by visible practices such as the Belonging Board that make connections collective rather than isolated. As belonging becomes embedded in daily practice, schools see stronger relationships, improved engagement, and accountability grounded in trust. This Way reinforces the chapter's central message: meaningful change for students experiencing poverty begins with adult design decisions, not student compliance.

What If?

What if there is no time to add one more thing? This concern is common in schools already managing competing priorities and limited capacity. The shift here is not about adding tasks but about changing how existing moments are used.

Connection can be embedded into routines that already exist—greeting students at the door, brief check-ins, intentional seating choices, or naming effort during instruction. When adults consistently lead with connection inside the time they already have, belonging becomes sustainable. Students notice the difference, and their willingness to engage grows. The research supports it, too.

If you have heard Adam speak, you will hear him say, "If I were superintendent of the world, I would require every teacher to stand outside their door and greet students daily." Why? Research shows that when teachers greet students at the door with brief, positive interactions, academic engagement increases by approximately twenty percent and disruptive behavior decreases by about nine percent, resulting in more instructional time on task (Cook et al., 2018). These findings suggest that greeting students is not an add-on, but a high-yield practice that strengthens learning conditions at the start of class (Cook et al., 2018).

Way 3 — Removing Barriers Through Systems of Support

What?

This Way shifts the work from individual effort to collective responsibility. Students experiencing poverty often face barriers far outside their control—transportation gaps, inconsistent access to food or health care, housing instability, and attendance disruptions that compound over time. When those barriers are treated as personal shortcomings, students are left to navigate systems that were never designed with their realities in mind.

Removing barriers is not about charity or rescue. It is about designing systems that anticipate predictable obstacles and respond with coordinated support. This Way calls on schools to move beyond isolated interventions and toward shared structures that identify barriers early, respond consistently, and reduce the friction that prevents students from fully accessing learning. When systems are designed to absorb challenges instead of amplifying them, students are more likely to attend, engage, and persist—even when circumstances remain complex.

Why?
Students experiencing poverty are disproportionately impacted when schools rely on individual resilience instead of systemic support. Transportation issues, medical appointments, housing transitions, and food insecurity do not occur sporadically; they are recurring realities that affect attendance and engagement in predictable ways. When schools fail to account for this, absences accumulate and learning gaps widen.

Research from the U.S. Department of Education (2024) indicates that chronic absenteeism among low-income students more than doubled following the pandemic, with transportation and basic-needs access cited as primary contributing factors. Attendance Works (2023) further reports that schools implementing coordinated wraparound support and community partnerships have seen attendance gains of up to twelve percentage points. These improvements are not the result of stricter policies or messaging campaigns—they come from systems that remove barriers before they become excuses.

There is often debate about whether schools should be addressing these challenges at all. Regardless of political landscape or philosophical stance, the reality remains: barriers to access are barriers to learning. If students are expected to thrive, schools must move past "this isn't our job" and design systems that meet students where they are. The cost of not doing so shows up in lost instructional time, disengagement, and inequitable outcomes that schools ultimately carry responsibility for addressing.

How?

Removing barriers requires intentional structures that make support visible, shared, and sustainable. These steps focus on adult coordination and system design rather than individual heroics.

1. Establish a Barrier-Breaker Team

Form a cross-functional team that includes teachers, counselors, administrators, and community liaisons. Charge the team with identifying recurring barriers and coordinating responses rather than reacting to individual cases. Meet regularly with a clear focus on patterns, not anecdotes.

2. Map Barriers Consistently

Use a recurring Barrier Mapping process to track common obstacles such as transportation delays, housing instability, medical needs, or food access. Document when barriers occur and how they affect attendance and engagement. Mapping patterns allows teams to move from surprise to anticipation.

3. Align Responses to Systems, Not Individuals

Develop consistent responses to recurring barriers so students are not dependent on who happens to notice or intervene. This may include adjusted schedules, transportation coordination, access to on-site resources, or flexible attendance supports. The goal is predictability for students and clarity for staff.

4. Leverage and Formalize Partnerships

Identify community partners—food banks, health clinics, after-school programs, transportation services—and clarify how and when they are activated. Move partnerships from informal favors to defined supports. When partnerships are formalized, access becomes equitable rather than incidental.

Reflection Prompts

- Which barriers most consistently interfere with attendance or engagement for students experiencing poverty?
- Where are we relying on individual effort instead of coordinated systems?
- How predictable are our responses when the same barrier shows up repeatedly?
- Which barriers do we notice quickly, and which ones remain invisible?

Then What?

In the short term, schools begin to see clearer patterns instead of recurring surprises. Attendance conversations shift from blame to problem-solving, and staff share responsibility for removing obstacles rather than managing consequences. Students experience fewer disruptions and more consistent access to instruction, even when challenges arise.

Over time, systems of support become embedded rather than reactive. Teams use shared tools, such as a **Resource 1.3 Barrier Breakers Dashboard** to monitor attendance, engagement, and support trends together instead of in isolation. Leaders use this information to allocate resources more strategically and refine partnerships. As barriers are reduced, students experience school as a place designed to support them, reinforcing the chapter's central theme that equity is built through intentional system design.

What If?

What if resources are limited or partnerships feel out of reach? This concern is common, especially in under-resourced communities. The starting point is not outside funding—it is clarity.

Begin by listening directly to students and families about the obstacles they face most often. Their lived experiences frequently surface low-cost, high-impact adjustments such as modified bus stops, flexible scheduling, or access to basic supplies on campus. When schools start with what is predictable and solvable, momentum builds—and systems begin to change one barrier at a time.

Way 4 — Empowering Families as Partners in Possibility

What?

Families experiencing poverty often engage with schools from a position of distance, caution, or past harm. This Way reframes family engagement as partnership rather than participation. Instead of asking families to adapt to school systems, it challenges schools to redesign their structures so families feel welcomed, respected, and empowered as contributors to their child's learning.

Empowering families does not mean adding more events or increasing attendance requirements. It means shifting power—recognizing families as experts on their children and honoring the strengths, knowledge, and resilience they bring. This Way focuses on creating accessible, relational systems that invite families into shared problem-solving and goal-setting. When schools treat families as partners in possibility rather than recipients of information, trust grows and student support becomes more coherent across home and school.

Why?

Families living in poverty often face barriers that make traditional school engagement difficult—nontraditional work hours, transportation challenges, language access, and prior experiences of feeling judged or unheard. When engagement is defined narrowly by attendance at meetings or events, schools unintentionally exclude the very families they most need to partner with.

Meta-analyses by Jeynes (2021) demonstrate that authentic family engagement is associated with significant gains in student achievement, attendance, and motivation. These gains are strongest when schools prioritize two-way communication and honor families' time, voices, and cultural contexts. Engagement that centers compliance or information delivery alone does not yield the same results.

When families are positioned as passive participants, opportunities for alignment and shared responsibility are lost. Schools may work hard, but work in parallel rather than partnership. Empowering families requires moving beyond invitations toward collaboration—creating systems in which families help shape goals, supports, and decisions. The risk of not doing this work is fragmentation: students navigating different expectations at home and school, and families disengaging from systems that feel inaccessible or unresponsive.

How?

Empowering families requires intentional adult decisions that lower barriers and redistribute voice. These steps focus on designing systems that make partnership possible and sustainable.

1. Lead With Listening Before Planning

Host listening opportunities designed around family schedules and locations, such as community "Listening Cafés" held in libraries, faith centers, apartment complexes, or virtual spaces. Use these sessions to hear families' priorities, concerns, and hopes without defending existing practices. Listening first signals respect and builds trust before solutions are proposed.

2. Redesign Access, Not Expectations

Provide communication and materials in families' home languages and use plain, clear language rather than educational jargon. Clarify how families can advocate for their child and who to contact when support is needed. Access improves when schools simplify pathways instead of expecting families to navigate complexity alone.

3. Co-Plan Meaningful Family–School Goals

Invite caregivers to co-design one shared goal per semester that connects home strengths to school growth. Frame goals around support and possibility rather than deficits. When families help define goals, alignment improves and follow-through becomes more consistent.

4. Normalize Relationship-Building as Core Work

Treat relationship-building with families as essential work rather than an extra task. Build time into calendars for follow-up conversations, check-ins, and shared reflection. Consistency matters more than scale when trust is the goal.

Reflection Prompts

- Whose voices are currently shaping our family engagement decisions, and whose are absent?
- Where have our systems prioritized convenience for the school over access for families?
- How often do families experience us listening without immediately explaining or fixing?
- In what ways are families positioned as partners rather than participants?

Then What?

In the short term, schools notice changes in tone and trust. Conversations with families become more open, and communication shifts from one-way updates to shared dialogue. Families begin to reach out earlier when challenges arise, and staff gain clearer insight into students' contexts and strengths outside of school.

Over time, family partnership becomes embedded in school culture rather than tied to individual staff members. Tools such as a Family Partnership Calendar help teams plan listening sessions, co-planning meetings, and resource events across the year, moving engagement beyond crisis response. **Resource 1.4: Family Partnership Calendar** supports this work by encouraging consistent, trust-building connections. As partnership deepens, students benefit from aligned expectations and shared belief across home and school.

Resource 1.4: Family Partnership Calendar Template

Month	Engagement Focus	Purpose (*Inform, Listen, Collaborate*)	Format(s) (*In-Person, Virtual, Home-Based*)	Primary Audience	Staff Lead	Follow-Up Action
September	Welcome & Relationship Building	Listen	In-Person	All Families	Admin Team	Summarize themes and share back
November	Learning Progress & Supports	Collaborate	Virtual	Families of Focus	Grade-Level Teams	Adjust support plans

What If?

What if turnout remains low or families seem hesitant to engage? This response is common and often reflects past experiences rather than lack of interest. Trust takes time, especially when families have learned to protect themselves from systems that previously felt unwelcoming.

Instead of asking families to come to school, bring school to the community. Attend neighborhood events, visit local laundromats, markets, or community centers, and show up in spaces where families already gather. When families see educators present without an agenda, relationships begin to shift. Over time, presence builds credibility—and partnership becomes possible.

Maya and Avery were not invisible in our system. In fact, they were clearly marked. Both twins appeared on our student data wall as Tier 2 for literacy—identified, tracked, discussed. Elena, because of her disability, was listed on our growth wall, where we monitored progress carefully and consistently. On paper, the system was working.

But poverty does not always announce itself through academic gaps alone. It shows up in the spaces between data points—in stamina, access, confidence, and stress that follows students quietly into classrooms. While we were watching their progress, we were missing their experience.

Our student data walls helped us identify needs, but they did not tell the full story. They didn't show how often materials were shared or missing, how enrichment opportunities felt out of reach, or how exhaustion and instability impacted focus and engagement. Because the twins were "Tier 2" and Elena was "on the growth list," we assumed the right supports were already in place. We monitored them well—but we did not design intentionally enough for the realities poverty brought into their daily learning.

What Maya, Avery, and Elena taught us is that systems built to track performance can still miss opportunity. When poverty is treated as a variable instead of a lived condition, schools' risk confusing intervention with impact. The result is a quiet kind of inequity—where students are discussed often, supported partially, and still left to navigate too much on their own.

Closing Reflection

When Jordan—the student from our opening vignette—returned to school a year later, things looked different. His counselor had connected his family with a community pantry. His teacher had restructured morning routines to include relationship check-ins. The school no longer viewed poverty as a deficit to remediate but as a context to understand and address collectively.

Jordan still faced challenges, but he also experienced moments of pride—seeing his name on the honor roll, hearing his teacher say, *"You're a leader here."*

The transformation didn't come from a single program or a heroic teacher. It came from a mindset shared across a community of educators who chose to see potential before problems. Poverty doesn't define a student's capacity to learn; it defines our opportunity to respond with courage, creativity, and care.

The Constellation of Learning™ Synopsis

This chapter embodies the theme of **Inclusive Excellence & Opportunity for All**, reminding us that equity is not a strategy but a mindset. When we view students through a lens of abundance rather than deficit, we begin to see their potential rather than their pain. Poverty is not a predictor of destiny—it is a context that demands compassion, creativity, and courage. Our role as educators is to dismantle the barriers that poverty builds and replace them with pathways that lead to agency and hope.

As we reflect on this constellation point, we must consider how inclusion becomes actionable through daily practice. Every classroom decision—how we group, assess, and support—either narrows or widens opportunity. By aligning our systems to the belief that every child deserves more than access—they deserve acceleration—we transform schools into communities where potential is not bound by circumstance.

Hallway Confessions – Daily Practice and Perspective

"I used to think I couldn't fix poverty," a sixth-grade teacher said quietly in a staff meeting. "Then I realized I wasn't supposed to fix it—I was supposed to *see* it."

She began keeping extra granola bars in her drawer, making morning check-ins part of routine attendance. Over time, her students stopped hiding hunger behind behavior. The class didn't magically become perfect, but the climate changed. Compassion became the classroom norm, and academic scores followed.

Small actions often spark the deepest shifts. Seeing a student fully is the most rigorous form of teaching we'll ever do.

The Dismissal Bell – The Five A's

When the final bell rings, the measure of our work is not what was taught, but whether every student had what they needed to learn with dignity. Poverty does not signal a lack of ability—it signals unmet conditions. Students leave our buildings each day carrying more than backpacks; they carry hunger, instability, and invisible stress that shape how learning is experienced.

When educators choose to design environments that anticipate need rather than react to crisis, schools become places of stability and possibility.

When educators choose to design environments that anticipate need rather than react to crisis, schools become places of stability and possibility. Equity begins when we stop asking students to overcome circumstances alone and start building systems that ensure access, care, and opportunity are not optional—but guaranteed.

Action Step	Description
Audit	Examine attendance, discipline, and course-failure data through a poverty lens. Identify structural inequities, not student deficits.
Adjust	Shift resources—time, staff, and funding—toward students and families facing the greatest barriers.
Advocate	Share stories of practice where student success is celebrated at board meetings and community events to build public will to ensure each student gets what they need at the right time at the right place.
Assemble	Form a cross-departmental equity team ("Barrier Breakers") that meets monthly to track and remove systemic obstacles.
Attitude Ask	What belief must we release to ensure every student in poverty experiences school as a place of abundance?

CHAPTER 2

Students with Disabilities: Redefining Ability Through Access and Advocacy

Opening Vignette

The classroom buzzed with quiet concentration as students gathered supplies for a group project on ecosystems. Eli, a fifth-grader with dyslexia and ADHD, shifted between excitement and dread. He loved building models, but reading directions was like walking through fog. When his teacher, Ms. Mendez, asked for volunteers to read aloud, Eli froze. Before she could call his name, his classmate Maya whispered, "I can read if you build." It was a small, instinctive gesture of equity—a peer creating access without a label attached.

Later, during cleanup, Ms. Mendez noticed the precision in Eli's model. She knelt beside him. "You know, the way you engineered this water-flow system is incredible," she said. His face lifted. She paused before adding, "Next time we read directions, let's use text-to-speech together so you can focus on building." The word *together* mattered more than the accommodation itself. For Eli, inclusion wasn't a plan written in a binder; it was a daily decision to be seen as capable.

This moment captures what every student with a disability needs—not lowered expectations or pity, but belief backed by intentional design. The words we choose, the tools we offer, and the mindsets we model either widen or close the distance between access and achievement.

What students with disabilities need first is not remediation, but recognition—recognition of their capacity, their voice, and their right to fully belong in spaces designed for learning. When schools talk about inclusion, the conversation often stops at access. But access alone does not guarantee belonging, dignity, or success. True inclusion isn't about fitting students into our plans—it's about expanding our plans until everyone fits.

> True inclusion isn't about fitting students into our plans—it's about expanding our plans until everyone fits.

Framing the Challenge

Today, more than 7.3 million students, or roughly fifteen percent of public-school enrollment, receive services under the Individuals with Disabilities Education Act (IDEA) (U.S. Department of Education, 2024). Post-pandemic research shows that students with disabilities experienced some of the steepest unfinished learning in both math and reading (NWEA, 2023). National Assessment of Educational Progress (NAEP) data from 2022 indicated that average reading scores for students with disabilities declined by four points since 2019, widening an already persistent gap.

Our son, Benjamin entered Kindergarten with an IEP stating he was to have a one-on-one paraprofessional at all times. Even though best practice would support that there be a consistent and familiar one-on-one paraprofessional with him, the reality was that he had a different one-on-one in the morning than he did in the afternoon. Granted his school followed the law; however, the practice was not best for him. What Ben needed was consistency. What they did not provide for him: consistency.

Although the law promises a *free appropriate public education*, many students still encounter limited inclusion, inconsistent support staff, and inaccessible materials. Staffing shortages in special education, particularly for paraprofessionals and related-service providers, have intensified since 2020 (Council for Exceptional Children, 2023). Educators report spending more time managing compliance paperwork than collaborating on instruction, and general-education teachers often express uncertainty about differentiation or modifications.

At the same time, families of students with disabilities are demanding more authentic partnership. Advocacy groups have amplified the call for culturally responsive evaluation and greater attention to the intersection of disability, race, and poverty. Federal data show that Black students are still more than twice as likely to be identified under emotional-disturbance categories than their White peers (Office for Civil Rights, 2023). These patterns remind us that equity requires vigilance, not assumption.

Educators face a complex challenge: provide individualized instruction while maintaining grade-level rigor and belonging. The shift from "pull-out support" to inclusive design is no longer optional—it is the future of effective schooling. Remember, it is ultimately up to the case conference team to determine the percentage of least restrictive environment for each child. Families and teachers should work collaboratively to maximize the amount of in-class time. Universal Design for Learning (UDL) offers a roadmap to get there.

Way 5 — Universal Design for Learning: Building Access from the Start

What?

Universal Design for Learning is an instructional design framework grounded in the neuroscience of how learners take in, process, and demonstrate understanding. Rather than retrofitting lessons after students struggle, UDL begins by anticipating learner variability from the start. It guides educators to plan multiple means of engagement, representation, and action and expression so access is built into instruction rather than added later (CAST, 2022).

For students with disabilities, this shift is foundational. UDL moves classrooms away from the idea that access is something provided to "some students" and toward the expectation that flexibility benefits everyone. It is not a special education initiative layered onto general instruction. It is a proactive approach to teaching that assumes learners will differ and designs accordingly. When access is planned upfront, students spend less time navigating barriers and more time engaging with meaningful learning.

Why?

Students with disabilities are often asked to adapt to instructional environments that were never designed with them in mind. When lessons rely on a single mode of instruction or expression, accommodations become the primary access point rather than a supplement. Over time, this can reinforce dependence, delay engagement, and unintentionally signal that access is an exception rather than a right.

UDL aligns with decades of research showing that proactive instructional design reduces barriers and improves outcomes for students with disabilities (Hattie, 2023). When instruction is designed from the margins inward, fewer reactive accommodations are required later. A 2024 meta-analysis by the National Center on Accessible Educational Materials found that classrooms implementing UDL principles reported twenty to twenty-five percent gains in engagement and task persistence among students with IEPs.

Beyond the data, UDL communicates a powerful message to students: we planned for you before you arrived. That message matters. It builds trust, supports belonging, and reinforces the idea that access is part of quality instruction, not a personal favor. When proactive design becomes the norm, tools such as **Resource 2.1: UDL Checkpoint Planning Guide** help educators anticipate and remove barriers before they limit access to learning.

How?

Implementing Universal Design for Learning requires intentional planning decisions that anticipate learner variability rather than reacting to barriers after they appear. The steps below focus on the specific actions educators and leaders take to design access from the start and sustain it through instruction and systems.

1. Anticipate learner variability during planning

Before teaching a unit, identify the cognitive, sensory, and linguistic demands of each task, then proactively embed flexible supports—such as visuals, audio options, sentence frames, or manipulatives—before instruction begins.

2. Design structured choice aligned to shared goals

Provide multiple ways for students to engage and demonstrate understanding—writing, oral explanation, video, or visual representation—while maintaining common learning targets and expectations.

3. Normalize accessibility as standard practice

Use captions, screen readers, translation tools, and accessible document formats as default features so access is predictable and embedded in classroom culture, not framed as an accommodation.

4. Align leadership systems to reinforce access and rigor

Embed UDL checkpoints into observation tools and professional learning plans so conversations about instructional quality consistently include access, not just outcomes.

5. Celebrate flexible design as instructional strength

Recognize and name effective UDL practices publicly to shift the narrative from compliance to creativity and reinforce access as a marker of strong teaching.

Reflection Prompts

- How often do my lessons require retrofitting after instruction has already begun?
- Where do students with disabilities encounter predictable barriers in my classroom?
- Which UDL principle feels most natural in my practice, and which requires more intentional planning?
- How might designing for the edges improve learning for students across the room?

Then What?

In the short term, classrooms become more responsive and less reactive. Students with disabilities engage more quickly, require fewer individual adjustments, and demonstrate greater persistence with challenging tasks. Teachers spend less time troubleshooting access issues and more time supporting learning.

Over time, UDL shifts instructional culture. Teams begin planning with variability in mind, and conversations about rigor expand to include access and flexibility. As proactive design spreads, schools reduce reliance on last-minute accommodations and build coherence between general and special education. Students experience learning environments where access is expected, reinforcing the chapter's focus on dignity, belonging, and high-quality instruction for students with disabilities.

What If?

What if colleagues worry that UDL adds more work? That concern is common and understandable. Begin by acknowledging that change often feels heavier before it feels more efficient, and share evidence that proactive design reduces reteaching and accommodation demands over time.

What if resources are limited? Start with mindset rather than materials. UDL's power lies in intentional planning and flexible thinking, not expensive tools. And if systems prioritize standardization over innovation, advocate for UDL within existing structures—curriculum adoption, professional growth plans, and evaluation frameworks—so access becomes the expectation rather than the exception.

Way 6 — Co-Teaching That Works: Shared Responsibility, Shared Wins

What?

Co-teaching is not simply two adults sharing the same classroom. It is the deliberate integration of expertise in which both educators share responsibility for planning, instruction, and outcomes. When implemented with intention, co-teaching blends the content expertise of the general education teacher with the specialized instructional knowledge of the special education teacher so that every student is viewed as *our* student.

The Individuals with Disabilities Education Act (IDEA) emphasizes placement in the least restrictive environment, but inclusion without collaboration often results in proximity rather than participation. True co-teaching redefines inclusion as intentional integration. It requires parity, trust, and shared ownership of student learning. When those conditions are present, students experience multiple access points without stigma, separation, or lowered expectations.

Why?

For students with disabilities, co-teaching can either expand access or quietly reinforce marginalization. When one teacher leads and the other assists, students quickly learn whose instruction "counts." This dynamic undermines inclusion and limits the instructional power of having two professionals in the room.

Research consistently shows that when co-teaching is implemented with fidelity, students with disabilities demonstrate stronger academic and social outcomes. A 2023 study from the Council for Exceptional Children found that students in co-taught classrooms scored an average of eight percentile points higher in reading fluency than peers in traditional pull-out settings. In addition, Friend and Cook (2023) found that teachers who planned together reported greater confidence in differentiation, classroom management, and instructional decision-making

Beyond academic gains, co-teaching shapes culture. When students see adults sharing authority, negotiating roles, and learning together, collaboration becomes normalized. Inclusion is no longer something done *for* students with disabilities; it becomes something modeled *with* them.

How?

Effective co-teaching depends on deliberate instructional choices and leadership support that make shared responsibility visible and sustainable. The steps below focus on adult decisions that move co-teaching from coordination to true collaboration.

1. Select the co-teaching model intentionally

Choose among station, parallel, alternative, or team-teaching models based on the instructional purpose of the lesson rather than convenience. **Resource 2.2: Co-Teaching Model Selector** supports teams in matching models to learning goals, while administrators reinforce this work by building schedules that allow for consistent partnerships and co-planning.

2. Protect shared planning time

Without joint planning, co-teaching becomes reactive rather than instructional. Even brief, protected planning windows allow teams to clarify learning goals, assessment criteria, and instructional roles before students enter the room.

3. Establish visible parity during instruction

Both educators should lead, question, and facilitate learning throughout the lesson rather than defaulting to one primary voice. Using shared language such as "we decided" or "our goal today" reinforces joint ownership and prevents role drift.

4. Reflect collaboratively after instruction

Co-teaching teams should regularly debrief what worked, which students benefited most, and where additional access points are needed. Reflection transforms collaboration into continuous professional learning rather than routine coordination.

5. Reinforce co-teaching as a core instructional strategy

School leaders must clearly communicate that co-teaching is not a supplemental service but an essential approach to instruction.

Providing joint professional learning and publicly recognizing effective teams strengthens shared responsibility and elevates practice.

Reflection Prompts

- How do students perceive the partnership between co-teachers in our classrooms?
- When are both educators equally engaged in instruction rather than one primarily assisting?
- What system conditions currently limit effective co-teaching in our building?
- How might co-teaching strengthen access beyond special education contexts?

Then What?

In the short term, classrooms become more dynamic and responsive. Students with disabilities receive instruction from two engaged educators rather than one primary teacher and one helper. Teachers report clearer roles, stronger alignment, and more effective differentiation during lessons.

Over time, co-teaching shifts school culture. Shared ownership becomes the norm, and instructional conversations move away from "my students" and "your students." As teams refine practice and share successes in PLCs, co-teaching becomes an expectation rather than an exception. This reinforces the chapter's focus on access, dignity, and high-quality instruction for students with disabilities.

What If?

What if one teacher feels overshadowed or underutilized? Address roles explicitly before instruction and establish norms for communication and feedback. Parity does not happen by accident; it is designed.

What if leaders resist allocating time for planning? Connect co-teaching to measurable outcomes rather than compliance. When co-teaching is framed as a growth strategy instead of a staffing decision, investment follows. And if students initially resist having two teachers, be transparent: learning happens in more than one way, and access improves when expertise is shared. Co-teaching thrives when adults model humility, trust, and shared accountability.

Way 7 — Data Conversations with Dignity: Using Progress Monitoring as Empowerment

What?

Progress monitoring is intended to guide instruction, yet for many students with disabilities it becomes a compliance routine disconnected from learning. Data is collected, entered, and reviewed, but rarely experienced as meaningful by the student whose name appears on the chart. This Way reframes progress monitoring as a tool for empowerment rather than diagnosis.

Progress monitoring includes formative checks, IEP goals, and classroom evidence that show how learning unfolds over time. The issue is not the absence of data, but how it is used and discussed. When data is framed around growth, strategies, and effort, it tells the story of a learner in motion rather than a label fixed in place. Data conversations with dignity ensure that information supports agency, belonging, and instructional clarity rather than compliance alone.

Why?

Students with disabilities often experience data as something done to them instead of something shared with them. Scores are reviewed in meetings they do not attend, language is deficit-oriented, and progress is discussed in terms of what is missing rather than what is developing. Over time, this can erode motivation and reinforce a sense that learning is measured *about* them, not *with* them.

Research from the National Center on Intensive Intervention (2024) found that students who participated in goal-setting and progress-monitoring conversations met growth targets thirty-five percent more frequently than peers who were unaware of their data. When students understand what they are working toward and how progress is measured, engagement and persistence increase.

Educators also benefit from shifting how data is discussed. Teachers who use strengths-based language when reviewing progress report fewer negative behavioral referrals and stronger student engagement. Reframing statements from "below benchmark" to "growing in comprehension stamina" changes how students see themselves as learners. Tools such as **Resource 2.3: Strengths-Based Learner Profile** help teams align supports around assets rather than gaps, reinforcing dignity while maintaining accountability.

How?

Data conversations that honor growth and dignity require intentional adult moves that keep progress visible, understandable, and actionable. The steps below focus on how educators and leaders design progress monitoring with students and families in ways that build ownership, trust, and momentum.

1. **Lead every data conversation with evidence of growth**
Begin reviews by naming specific gains, even when progress is incremental, to establish momentum before identifying next steps and areas for continued focus.
2. **Make data visually accessible to students**
Translate complex graphs into clear visuals such as color-coded trackers or goal thermometers, and invite students to interact with their data so ownership is shared rather than symbolic.

3. Schedule regular micro-conferences

Use short, five-minute weekly check-ins to keep feedback timely and relational, ensuring progress monitoring functions as dialogue rather than judgment.

4. Engage families as partners in the process

Share plain-language summaries that highlight growth trends and next goals instead of isolated scores, helping families see progress and align support.

5. Model growth-centered data practices through leadership

Structure data meetings to begin with student growth stories and reflective questions, reinforcing progress and resilience as central to improvement. **Resource 2.4: Data with Dignity Template** supports teams in maintaining growth-focused conversations without losing instructional clarity.

Reflection Prompts

- When reviewing data, do I begin with strengths or gaps?
- How often are students directly involved in understanding their own progress?
- What language patterns show up in my data conversations?
- How could our team redesign data meetings to reinforce dignity and agency?

Then What?

In the short term, students become more aware of their goals and more invested in progress. Conferences feel collaborative rather than corrective, and students engage more actively in monitoring their own growth. Teachers report clearer instructional decisions and stronger relationships with students and families.

Over time, progress monitoring becomes a shared responsibility rather than a reporting requirement. Schools develop a culture in which data is used to guide instruction, celebrate growth, and plan next steps with students at the center. This Way reinforces the chapter's emphasis on access and dignity by ensuring that data supports learning without reducing students to numbers.

What If?

What if time constraints make individual conferences difficult? Consider asynchronous options such as brief voice notes or short video reflections that review progress. These approaches maintain connection without adding meetings.

What if colleagues worry that dignity-focused data conversations reduce rigor? Clarify that accountability and affirmation are not opposites. Naming growth strengthens persistence and supports higher expectations. If data systems feel overwhelming, start with one meaningful indicator and expand intentionally. When data honors humanity, students see themselves not as charts, but as learners with direction and agency.

Way 8 — Building a Culture of Belonging: From Compliance to Connection

What?

Inclusion is not defined by placement alone; it is defined by culture. A school can meet every compliance requirement and still fail to create a sense of belonging for students with disabilities. Belonging grows when educators move beyond policies and procedures and attend to how students experience daily interactions, language, and routines.

Students know the difference between being accommodated and being embraced. That difference shows up in whether their presence feels expected or merely allowed. Schools that build a culture of belonging do not simply make room for differences; they design learning environments around them. This Way focuses on shifting from compliance-driven inclusion to connection-driven belonging, where students with disabilities experience school as a place they are known, valued, and integral to the community.

Why?

Belonging is a strong predictor of student success. The 2023 Gallup Education Index reported that students who felt known and valued at school were 2.6 times more likely to meet grade-level benchmarks in reading and mathematics. For students with disabilities, belonging often determines whether they persist academically and socially or withdraw over time.

When belonging is present, students internalize a message of capability rather than charity. Accessibility tools become normalized, peer relationships strengthen, and responsibility for inclusion is shared rather than isolated. When belonging is absent, even well-designed supports can feel stigmatizing. Policies may technically include students, but daily experiences quietly communicate exclusion. Building a culture of belonging ensures that access is paired with dignity and that inclusion is experienced, not just documented.

How?

A culture of belonging is created through intentional adult actions that are modeled, reinforced, and repeated across classrooms and common spaces. The steps below focus on what educators and leaders do to make belonging visible, relational, and shared throughout the school community.

1. Model inclusive language in all settings

Pay close attention to how students are referenced in classrooms, meetings, and informal conversations, shifting from distancing language to shared ownership that reinforces dignity and communicates collective responsibility.

2. Teach peers about learner variability

Use age-appropriate activities to highlight strengths, empathy, and differences in how people learn so variability is understood as normal rather than exceptional.

3. Broaden how success is recognized and celebrated

Acknowledge creativity, persistence, collaboration, and growth alongside academic achievement to expand students' understanding of what it means to belong and succeed.

4. Strengthen peer connections through intentional structures

Implement cross-age mentoring, peer support groups, or circle-of-friends models to reduce isolation and build shared responsibility for inclusion.

5. Examine the environment through a belonging lens

Use tools such as **Resource 2.5: Belonging Audit Tool** to review daily language, visuals, and routines and assess how inclusion is experienced across the school.

Reflection Prompts

- What messages do our hallways, announcements, and celebrations send about who belongs?
- Which students might feel invisible within our current routines?
- How am I intentionally designing for belonging in tomorrow's lesson?
- Where does our definition of success need to expand?

Then What?

In the short term, schools notice shifts in tone and interaction. Students with disabilities participate more fully, peer relationships strengthen, and classroom communities feel more connected.

Educators become more aware of how language, routines, and recognition shape student experience.

Over time, belonging becomes embedded in school culture rather than dependent on individual staff members. Leaders use tools such as belonging audits to refine practices, representation, and communication. As shared ownership deepens, inclusion moves from compliance to connection, reinforcing the chapter's emphasis on dignity, access, and community for students with disabilities.

What If?

What if staff worry that focusing on belonging detracts from academics? Connection precedes cognition. Students learn more effectively when they feel safe, seen, and significant, and belonging strengthens rather than replaces rigor.

What if families or community members misunderstand inclusion as lowering standards? Communicate clearly that inclusion raises expectations by designing learning environments where excellence is accessible to all. Belonging is not extra kindness; it is equity in action.

Closing Reflection – "The Gift of Time and Trust"

When Eli returned to Ms. Mendez's class the following year, he brought with him a sense of ease that wasn't there before. He volunteered to read during the morning meeting—slowly, carefully, with his tablet narrating the words alongside him. The class listened, then applauded. Ms. Mendez didn't see an accommodation; she saw growth born from trust.

Every educator holds the power to create moments like these—moments when inclusion feels like air, not effort. Building systems for students with disabilities takes time, patience, and courage. But when we plan for all from the start, when we co-teach with purpose, when we humanize data and center belonging, time gives us back something precious: every learner's voice.

The Constellation of Learning™ Synopsis

This chapter connects deeply to **Instructional Coherence & High-Quality Teaching**, revealing how intentional design ensures students with disabilities experience belonging, not separation. When instruction aligns to shared goals, structures, and supports, learners of all abilities thrive within the same ecosystem of excellence. This coherence gives every student access to rigor and relevance rather than remediation and removal.

Educators are not simply providers of accommodation—they are architects of possibility. Each modification or scaffold should preserve dignity and spark independence. When coherence guides our work, we move from "doing for" to "learning with," creating a system where every child's strengths become the foundation of collective growth.

Hallway Confessions – Daily Practice & Perspective

It's the small things that stay with us: the teacher who learns to silence their perfectionism and celebrate partial progress; the paraeducator who advocates for a voice amplifier because whispering isn't inclusion; the student who quietly says, "Thanks for letting me use my iPad — I finally feel smart again."

There are days when fatigue wins. Paperwork piles high, patience runs low, and the temptation to revert to compliance grows. But then a student's smile, a family's gratitude, or a colleague's breakthrough reminds us that inclusion is holy work — messy, human, and worth every ounce of effort.

The Dismissal Bell – The Five A's

When the final bell rings, the question is not whether accommodations were provided—but whether students were truly able to participate, belong, and grow. Compliance may satisfy a checklist, but it does not guarantee dignity. Too often, students with disabilities leave classrooms having received support that limits independence or lowers expectation rather than expands access. When educators design for variability from the start, supports become bridges instead of barriers. True inclusion is not about doing enough to meet the law; it is about creating learning environments in which students with disabilities are seen as capable, valued contributors whose success is expected—not managed.

Action Step	Description
Audit	Examine your schedules, lesson plans, and data conversations. Where are students with disabilities still experiencing barriers?
Adjust	Redesign one system—grading, intervention time, or communication—to make it more accessible and inclusive.
Advocate	Use your influence to ensure that students with disabilities are represented in leadership opportunities, student councils, and advanced classes.
Assemble	Form a cross-role inclusion team that meets monthly to monitor progress and celebrate growth.
Attitude Ask	Approach every conversation about students with disabilities with one guiding belief: *We planned for you before you arrived.* Let that belief guide how you teach, lead, and love.

CHAPTER 3

Students Experiencing Homelessness: Restoring Stability, Dignity, and Hope

Opening Vignette

When eighth-grader Jasmine stepped into her classroom that fall, she carried no backpack, no supplies—just a quiet kind of exhaustion behind her smile. Her hair was pulled back with a twist tie, her hoodie sleeves stretched past her hands, and her eyes scanned the room as if she were waiting for something to go wrong. By week two her teacher learned she was staying in a family shelter. Transportation was inconsistent. Homework was never turned in. But she showed up—and that's where we began redefining what success looked like.

Jasmine's story isn't rare. Every day, students walk through school doors carrying burdens invisible to most: fear, instability, or the fatigue that comes from constant transition. For many, school is the only steady place in their lives—the one space where the lights always come on, a meal is guaranteed, and an adult remembers their name.

Framing the Challenge

For too many students experiencing homelessness, school represents more than academics; it is their primary source of stability. According to the National Center for Homeless Education (2024), more than 1.5 million students across the United States were identified as experiencing homelessness during the 2022–2023 school year—a fourteen percent increase from the previous year. These students include children living in shelters, doubled-up with other families, in motels, cars, or temporary spaces rarely visible to educators, yet deeply disruptive to learning.

The data reveal additional complexity. Roughly one in five students experiencing homelessness is also identified with a disability, and one in five is an English learner (NCHE, 2024). Racial disparities persist: 39 percent identify as Hispanic or Latino, 25 percent as Black, and 25 percent as White (NCHE, 2024). These overlapping factors compound barriers—transportation, digital access, and social-emotional health—making it even harder for students to stay engaged.

The Institute for Children, Poverty, and Homelessness (2023) reports that homeless students are twice as likely to be suspended, four times more likely to drop out, and often two to three grade levels behind their peers. These statistics don't reflect capability; they expose inequity.

We may not control where a student sleeps at night, but we absolutely control how they are treated at 8:05 a.m. Ensuring each student has what they need begins with access—and access starts with belonging. It's time to move on from asking, *"What's wrong with this student?"* to *"What barriers are in their way, and how do we remove them?"*

Before academic judgments are made, **Resource 3.1: Student Stability Snapshot** helps educators understand the conditions shaping a student's learning experience. But, before we talk about achievement, engagement, or accountability, we must be honest about what learning requires at its core. For students whose lives are marked by instability or fear, safety is not an add-on—it is the foundation. Safety is the first curriculum; only when students feel secure do their hearts and minds open to possibility.

> Safety is the first curriculum; only when students feel secure do their hearts and minds open to possibility.

Resource 3.1: Stability & Access Tracker

Student / Group	Stability Indicator	Observed Change	Impact on Learning	Support or Adjustment	Follow-Up Date
Student A	Attendance	Increase in absences	Missed instructional time	Provide flexible make-up options	10/15
Student B	Transportation	Route change	Late arrival to class	Coordinate adjusted schedule	10/22

Way 9 — Build Stability Through Ritual, Not Rigidity

What?

Students experiencing homelessness often navigate lives shaped by unpredictability—frequent moves, changing caregivers, inconsistent access to basic needs, and shifting daily routines. In that context, traditional school structures meant to create order can feel overwhelming or punitive rather than supportive. This Way distinguishes between rigidity and ritual, emphasizing stability built through relational consistency rather than inflexible compliance.

Rituals are intentional, human-centered practices that repeat with purpose. A daily check-in question, a consistent greeting at the door, a shared moment of reflection, or a predictable classroom opening all function as anchors. These moments communicate safety, recognition, and belonging. Unlike rigid routines that demand conformity, rituals offer reassurance. They transform repetition into connection and signal to students, "You are expected here, and this place is steady—even when life is not."

Why?

For students experiencing homelessness, predictability is not a preference; it is a protective factor. When housing, transportation, and family circumstances change frequently, the nervous system remains on high alert. Chronic uncertainty elevates stress responses that interfere with attention, memory, and emotional regulation.

Neuroscience research shows that trauma increases cortisol levels and narrows cognitive capacity, while predictable, positive routines help regulate stress and reopen pathways for learning (Perry & Winfrey, 2021). In school settings, small, consistent adult actions—such as a warm greeting, a predictable transition, or a familiar opening activity—become powerful stabilizers. They send a clear message that school is a safe and reliable space.

Without these stabilizing practices, students may appear disengaged, guarded, or resistant. Those behaviors are often misread as defiance rather than survival. Rituals counter that misinterpretation by reducing anxiety and rebuilding trust over time. When stability is embedded into the school day through relational practices, students are better positioned to engage academically and socially.

How?

Stability through ritual is created intentionally and sustained through consistent adult actions that prioritize predictability without rigidity. The steps below focus on how educators and leaders design simple, repeatable practices that help students feel grounded and secure.

1. Introduce one small, consistent ritual

Select a brief practice that can be sustained daily—such as a question of the day, a mindful minute, or a consistent class opening—so reliability is established without overwhelming students or staff.

2. Use visual anchors to reduce uncertainty

Post daily agendas, picture schedules, or transition cues to help students anticipate what comes next and regain a sense of control when other aspects of life feel unpredictable.

3. Name the ritual and protect its consistency

Give the practice a clear name, such as "Morning Launch" or "Community Circle," and maintain it over time to build familiarity, anticipation, and trust.

4. Celebrate continuity rather than perfection.

Acknowledge when rituals are sustained across days or weeks and name that consistency as a shared accomplishment, reinforcing collective ownership and reliability.

Reflection Prompts

- Which moments in our school day already provide predictability and calm for students?
- Where might rigid routines be unintentionally increasing stress?
- How can we make transitions more relational without adding time?

- What rituals could we protect even during busy or disrupted days?

Then What?

In the short term, students begin to arrive more regulated and engaged. Classrooms feel calmer, transitions become smoother, and students participate more freely. Educators notice fewer emotional escalations and stronger connections, particularly with students who previously appeared guarded or withdrawn.

Over time, rituals become part of the school's culture rather than individual classroom practices. Students begin to rely on predictable moments of connection, and trust deepens. As ownership grows, students may even suggest or lead rituals themselves, reinforcing agency and belonging. This Way supports the chapter's focus on stability as a foundation for learning for students experiencing homelessness.

What If?

What if students seem resistant or disengaged at first? Hold steady. Trust develops through repetition, not intensity, and some students need time to test whether consistency will last.

Offer choice within rituals to preserve agency—such as selecting how to greet or participate. When rituals remain predictable yet flexible, control is shared and safety grows. Over time, these practices become the heartbeat of belonging rather than another requirement to endure.

Way 10 — Make Invisible Needs Visible— Without the Spotlight

What?

Students experiencing homelessness often rely on resilience, adaptability, and discretion to move through their school day. Many work intentionally to conceal their circumstances, not wanting to be singled out, pitied, or exposed. This Way focuses on designing school environments where support is normalized and readily available so students never have to ask for help or explain their situation.

The goal is not to identify need publicly; it is to remove stigma entirely. When classrooms and common spaces are stocked with open-access supplies, snacks are available without permission, and flexible learning options are quietly embedded, support becomes part of the environment rather than a special accommodation. Dignity-centered design shifts schools from scarcity thinking to sufficiency, ensuring that care is experienced as routine rather than remedial.

Why?

When basic survival needs compete with schooling, learning becomes secondary. Students who are hungry, worried about clothing, or unsure where they will sleep are expending cognitive energy simply to get through the day. Research from the Institute for Children, Poverty, and Homelessness (2023) found that consistent, discreet access to food, clothing, and hygiene items increased attendance rates by nearly thirty percent among students experiencing homelessness.

For school leaders, compassion must be systemic rather than situational. Reliance on individual discretion or goodwill creates uneven access and reinforces stigma. Policies that guarantee participation in transportation, meal programs, and extracurricular activities—without burdensome documentation—signal belonging. Collaboration with a district's McKinney-Vento liaison ensures that flexibility and confidentiality coexist, protecting students' rights while preserving dignity.

When supports are visible but non-stigmatizing, students reclaim cognitive capacity for learning. They engage more fully because the environment communicates a clear message: support is here for everyone, and you do not have to justify your need.

How?

Supporting students with invisible needs requires intentional environmental and policy design that removes barriers without drawing attention. The steps below focus on adult actions that normalize access, protect dignity, and embed compassion into daily systems rather than individual discretion.

1. Normalize access to support for all students

Stock classrooms, offices, and shared spaces with supplies that any student may use without explanation so help-seeking is universal and students experiencing homelessness are not singled out.

2. Design spaces for dignity rather than control

Use open shelves, clearly labeled but non-identifying bins, or "take what you need" stations instead of locked closets or sign-out systems to communicate trust and belonging through physical design.

3. Build and sustain community partnerships

Partner with local businesses, faith-based organizations, and community agencies to maintain supplies and ensure support is consistent, reliable, and not dependent on crisis response.

4. Align policies with empathy and flexibility

Review attendance, grading, and participation procedures through an equity lens and build flexibility into written expectations.

Resource 3.2: Dignity-Centered Classroom Flexibility Menu

supports educators in offering access without requiring disclosure, ensuring compassion is embedded into systems.

Reflection Prompts
* How does our environment signal that support is available to everyone?
* Where might students still feel exposed or singled out when accessing help?
* Which policies unintentionally create barriers to participation?
* How could community partnerships strengthen our network of care?

Then What?

In the short term, students begin using available supports more freely and with less hesitation. Attendance stabilizes, participation increases, and students spend less energy managing fear of exposure. Educators notice that when access is predictable and discreet, students engage more consistently in learning.

Over time, trust deepens. Students begin taking initiative without prompting, a sign that the system feels safe and reliable. Leaders use usage patterns and anonymous feedback to refine supports and ensure equity of access. As dignity-centered design becomes part of school culture, support is no longer a signal of need—it is a shared norm.

What If?

What if students still avoid resources? Reframe the narrative publicly and consistently. Use language that emphasizes community care rather than charity, and ensure messaging reflects shared ownership.

If concerns arise about misuse or cost, return to purpose. The goal is not perfect control but equitable access. When systems prioritize dignity, students learn that school is a place where their humanity is protected and their learning can take priority.

Way 11 — Empower Staff to Act with Compassion, Not Assumption

What?

Students experiencing homelessness often display behaviors that are easy to misinterpret. Fatigue, tardiness, irritability, inconsistent attendance, or unfinished work can quickly be labeled as defiance, disengagement, or lack of effort. This Way challenges schools to interrupt that reflex and replace assumption with understanding.

Empowering staff to act with compassion does not mean excusing behavior or lowering expectations. It means grounding responses in context rather than character. When educators pause to ask, "What happened?" instead of "What's wrong?" they open the door to connection and problem-solving. This Way focuses on building adult capacity to respond with curiosity, care, and consistency so students experiencing homelessness encounter school as a place of safety rather than judgment.

Why?

For students navigating housing instability, school can either be a stabilizing force or another source of stress. When adult responses default to punishment or exclusion, students receive the message that their circumstances make them a problem to manage. Over time, those interactions erode trust and increase disengagement.

Research consistently points to the power of relational safety. The Substance Abuse and Mental Health Services Administration identifies the presence of at least one caring adult as a key protective factor for youth facing adversity (SAMHSA, 2022). When educators respond with patience and empathy, students are more likely to regulate emotions, remain connected to school, and persist through challenges.

> Compassion becomes contagious when it is modeled, supported, and recognized.

Schools that intentionally build compassionate practice also see system-level benefits. Educators report fewer disciplinary referrals, calmer classrooms, and stronger relationships with students and families. Compassion becomes contagious when it is modeled, supported, and recognized. Without intentional structures, however, empathy remains inconsistent—dependent on individual disposition rather than shared expectation. This Way ensures compassion is taught, practiced, and sustained as part of professional culture.

How?

Designing access systems that students actually use requires intentional messaging, flexible structures, and a clear commitment to dignity over control. When barriers persist, leaders respond not by retreating, but by refining how care is communicated and enacted.

1. Reframe the Narrative Publicly

Use consistent language that centers community care rather than charity. Ensure all messaging—announcements, signage, staff conversations, and family communication—reflects shared ownership and collective responsibility.

2. Normalize Use Through Visibility

Integrate access points into everyday school routines so support is seen as expected, not exceptional. When resources are embedded into the rhythm of the school day, stigma diminishes.

3. Respond to Resistance with Purpose, Not Policing

If concerns arise about misuse or cost, return to the core purpose of the system. The goal is not perfect control, but equitable access aligned to student needs.

4. Protect Dignity Through Design

Examine how students encounter supports—from location to language to process. Systems that prioritize dignity signal to students that their humanity is protected and their learning can take priority

Reflection Prompts

- When have we reacted before fully understanding a student's context?
- Which behaviors are most likely to trigger assumptions in our building?
- ⊠How do our systems allow time for conversation rather than immediate consequence?
- In what ways do we hold one another accountable for compassionate responses?

Then What?

In the short term, classrooms become calmer and more predictable. Students experience fewer confrontational interactions and are more willing to communicate needs. Educators report greater confidence in responding to challenging behavior without escalating situations.

Over time, compassionate practice becomes embedded in school culture. Discipline data reflects fewer referrals and suspensions, while relationships strengthen across classrooms. During transitions that often disrupt support, tools such as **Resource 3.3: Continuity of Care Communication Protocol** help ensure that understanding and information travel with the student rather than resetting expectations. As compassion becomes a shared standard, students experiencing homelessness encounter school as a place that responds with humanity and consistency.

What If?

What if skepticism arises about whether compassion is effective? Begin with storytelling and proximity. Invite staff to hear directly from students, liaisons, or counselors who can contextualize behaviors and needs. Empathy grows when experiences are humanized rather than abstract.

If concerns surface about maintaining expectations, clarify that compassion and accountability coexist. Understanding context strengthens, rather than weakens, instructional response. When adults act with informed compassion, students are more likely to stay engaged—and schools become places where resilience is nurtured rather than tested.

Way 12 — Foster Connection and Belonging Through Mentorship

What?

For students experiencing homelessness, belonging often begins with one consistent adult who notices them, checks in, and follows through. Mentorship—whether formal or informal—creates that bridge. It may look like a teacher who checks in weekly, a counselor who consistently asks how the day is going, or a staff member who remembers a student's interests and story. These steady interactions create predictability in a life often marked by change.

Mentorship extends beyond academic support. It establishes emotional safety and communicates that relationships can endure even when circumstances outside of school are unstable. When adults show up consistently, students receive a powerful message: you matter here, and you are not invisible. This Way focuses on building intentional systems so mentorship is reliable, equitable, and sustained rather than left to chance.

Why?

Belonging is a critical driver of engagement and persistence. Research from the Search Institute (2023) found that students who could identify at least one trusted adult at school were three times more likely to attend regularly and twice as likely to report motivation to learn. For students experiencing homelessness, that trusted relationship often becomes the anchor that keeps them connected to school during periods of disruption.

Without intentional mentorship, students may move through a building unnoticed, especially during transitions or frequent absences. When no adult is clearly responsible for connection, gaps emerge. Mentorship counters that risk by ensuring every student has at least one person who notices changes, follows up, and advocates when needed. Over time, those relationships strengthen trust, stabilize attendance, and reinforce a sense of belonging that supports learning.

How?

Effective mentorship must be intentionally designed at the system level and sustained through shared responsibility. When mentorship is treated as a core structure rather than an informal practice, schools can ensure every student is meaningfully connected to a caring adult.

1. Establish a Structured Mentorship Model

Pair trained staff mentors with students identified through McKinney-Vento supports, counselor referrals, or attendance and engagement data. Set clear expectations for mentors, including purpose, frequency of contact, and documentation of check-ins to maintain consistency.

2. Expand Mentorship Through Peer Connections

Incorporate near-peer mentoring by training older students to support younger peers. Emphasize empathy, confidentiality, and relationship-building to reduce isolation and strengthen a sense of belonging.

3. Monitor Adult Connections Intentionally

Ensure every student can name at least one trusted adult in the building. Use surveys or staff-student mapping to identify students without a clear connection, and assign mentors proactively rather than waiting for concerns to escalate.

4. Protect Time for Relationship-Building

Prioritize short, consistent interactions—such as weekly fifteen-minute meetings or brief daily check-ins. Consistency, not intensity, builds trust and sustains meaningful relationships.

Reflection Prompts

- How do we currently ensure that every student has a trusted adult connection?
- Which students might be moving through our building without a clear mentor?
- How can mentorship be embedded into daily routines rather than added as an extra task?
- What structures help sustain relationships during transitions or absences?

Then What?

In the short term, students begin to show stronger attendance and engagement. They are more likely to seek help, communicate challenges, and remain connected during periods of instability.

Educators report clearer insight into student needs and stronger relational confidence.

Over time, mentorship becomes part of school culture rather than an isolated initiative. Stories of connection are shared, reinforcing purpose and collective responsibility. Tools such as **Resource 3.4: Trusted Adult Assignment Tracker** help schools formalize relational stability so no student is overlooked. As mentorship systems mature, belonging deepens and support becomes more equitable.

What If?

What if momentum fades or mentors feel stretched? Recognition matters. Publicly celebrating mentorship keeps relational work visible and valued. Ongoing training and reflection help sustain commitment.

When students require additional support, wraparound services and family involvement become essential. Difficult conversations must be handled with care to preserve trust. **Resource 3.5: Family Dignity Conversation Guide** supports communication that centers respect and partnership. Belonging grows when mentorship extends beyond one relationship into a network of care.

For a period of time, Maya, Avery, and Elena experienced housing instability—something we did not initially know. Their transition didn't come with announcements or visible signs. They still showed up. They still smiled. They still tried. And because they were quiet about it, the system stayed quiet, too.

Homelessness often hides behind normalcy. When schools wait for disclosure instead of designing for dignity, students bear the burden of asking for help they may not know how to request. The girls didn't need sympathy—they needed systems that assumed instability was possible and responded with flexibility, grace, and consistency. What we learned too late was that invisibility does not mean absence of need.

Closing Reflection

There is no single solution to homelessness, but there is extraordinary power in ensuring that when a student walks into school, they feel seen, safe, and valued. We can't guarantee a stable home, but we can guarantee stability within our walls. Each warm greeting, flexible deadline, and patient response tells students, *You belong here.*

The heart of this work isn't programs; it's presence. Each time we replace assumption with empathy, we rebuild faith in what school can represent—safety, hope, and possibility. Belonging doesn't start with the system. It starts with us.

The Constellation of Learning™ Synopsis

Grounded in **Whole-School & Community Well-Being**, this chapter calls us to recognize that students experiencing homelessness need more than empathy—they need ecosystems of safety. Stability begins with trust, and trust begins when adults refuse to define children by their living situations. When we stabilize a child's sense of belonging, academic growth follows naturally.

This constellation reminds us that well-being is both personal and institutional. Schools that thrive extend care beyond the classroom—partnering with families, agencies, and communities to rebuild consistency where chaos once existed. When the environment becomes predictable, students can finally release the energy spent surviving and redirect it toward learning.

Hallway Confessions – Daily Practice and Perspective

Addressing homelessness is both a moral and practical imperative. When basic needs go unmet, learning cannot flourish. Prioritizing our most vulnerable students doesn't dilute rigor; it defines it. One teacher with whom we worked put it best: *"When we cared for our students living in motels, attendance improved for everyone."* Compassion strengthens the entire culture.

The Dismissal Bell – The Five A's

When the final bell rings, some students leave knowing exactly where they will sleep—and others do not. For students experiencing homelessness, school is often the most stable place in an otherwise unpredictable life. Our responsibility, then, is not simply to provide instruction, but to protect continuity, dignity, and access without requiring explanation or exposure. When educators design systems that anticipate disruption and quietly remove barriers, students are free to focus on learning rather than survival. Stability is not created through sympathy or exception—it is built through intentional practices that ensure no student has to choose between being supported and being seen.

Action Step	Description
Audit	Review current systems: Do we know how many students experience homelessness? Where are the gaps?
Adjust	Revise policies that unintentionally penalize instability—attendance, dress code, deadlines.
Advocate	Use your influence to elevate awareness and connect with local service agencies.
Assemble	Form a multidisciplinary support team that meets monthly to coordinate care.
Attitude Ask	When students enter our spaces, let them feel seen before they're tested, heard before they're graded, valued before they're corrected. Belonging starts with our belief in them.

Students from Undocumented Homes: Learning Without Fear, Leading Without Borders

Opening Vignette

Marisol had practiced her lines for the eighth-grade play for weeks, her script covered in doodles of hearts and stars. But the permission slip to participate sat unsigned in her backpack, folded so many times it was soft around the edges. Every morning she watched her classmates drop theirs in the teacher's basket; every afternoon, she tucked hers deeper between her notebooks.

When her teacher finally asked about it, Marisol whispered that her mother hadn't had time. The truth was more complicated. Her mother, Lucía, feared that any form—any paper bearing her name—could expose the family's undocumented status. They'd come to the United States when Marisol was two, chasing safety and work. For twelve years they'd built a quiet life, but every new document still felt like a risk.

That night, Lucía stood at the kitchen counter tracing the edges of the slip. "Will they ask for my ID?" she murmured in Spanish. "No, Mamá," Marisol promised, though she wasn't certain. Together they filled in the lines carefully, stopping when they reached the signature line. "Maybe tomorrow," Lucía said, setting the paper aside.

The next morning, the permission slip stayed at home. Marisol didn't make it to rehearsal that week, and when the curtain rose on opening night, her seat in the front row remained empty. No one in the audience knew that fear—not talent—had kept her away.

In classrooms across the country, thousands of students like Marisol navigate school experiences shadowed by the quiet anxiety of documentation status. Their stories, often untold, reveal the hidden barriers that shape opportunity and belonging.

Framing the Challenge

The United States is home to more than eleven million undocumented immigrants, including approximately 1.9 million children living in mixed-status families—where at least one family member is undocumented (Pew Research Center, 2023). In schools, these families represent a unique population of students who often face both academic and emotional obstacles rooted in fear, stigma, and uncertainty about their future. According to the Migration Policy Institute (2024), nearly 5.2 million K–12 students in the U.S. have at least one undocumented parent. For educators, this means that in almost every district—and in nearly every classroom—students like Marisol are present, though their circumstances are seldom discussed openly.

While the Supreme Court's 1982 decision in *Plyler v. Doe* guaranteed that all children, regardless of immigration status, have the right to a free public education, that protection doesn't erase the daily barriers undocumented families face. Fear of deportation, language differences, limited access to healthcare and technology, and exclusion from many social programs can all hinder academic engagement and attendance (Gándara & Ee, 2021). These challenges often intensify during transitions between schools, as families move frequently in search of stability or safety.

In recent years, shifts in immigration policy and public rhetoric have amplified stress among undocumented and mixed-status households. A 2022 study by the UCLA Center for the Transformation of Schools found that 68% of educators reported seeing heightened anxiety, absenteeism, or withdrawal among students from undocumented homes following high-profile immigration enforcement events. Such chronic stress impacts learning and emotional regulation—key components of cognitive growth and academic success.

Yet despite these challenges, schools remain a powerful refuge. When educators cultivate trust, affirm identity, and remove unnecessary bureaucratic barriers, they can transform the classroom into a space of belonging rather than fear. This chapter explores how intentional practices—grounded in empathy, policy awareness, and advocacy—can help every child, regardless of documentation status, access the full promise of public education

Way 13 — Creating a Culture of Trust in Every Classroom

What?

Creating a culture of trust for students from undocumented homes begins with one essential belief: safety must precede learning. Trust is not built through a single welcoming message or poster; it is formed through the steady accumulation of daily actions that communicate consistency, care, and protection. When students believe their stories are safe, learning becomes possible.

For students whose families live with ongoing fear of exposure or separation, even routine school questions can trigger anxiety.

Building trust requires intentional choices about what information is collected, how it is discussed, and how confidentiality is protected. When educators design classroom routines and communication practices that honor privacy, affirm cultural identity, and center belonging, students learn not only content but that their presence matters as much as their performance.

Why?

Students from undocumented homes often experience what psychologists describe as "toxic vigilance"—a heightened state of alertness caused by chronic fear of exposure, detention, or family separation (Suárez-Orozco et al., 2023). This vigilance can shape how students engage with authority figures and institutions, including schools.

According to the American Psychological Association (2022), prolonged fear and uncertainty interfere with executive functioning, attention, and working memory—skills directly connected to learning readiness. For adolescents, this stress may surface as disengagement or defiance, behaviors frequently misinterpreted as apathy rather than self-protection.

Trust mitigates these effects. When schools adopt trauma-informed practices that emphasize safety, predictability, and voice, students from undocumented homes show higher attendance, stronger engagement, and greater resilience (Olsen & Martínez, 2022). Trust also extends to families. When caregivers believe a school will protect sensitive information, they are more likely to engage in conferences, complete forms, and participate in decision-making (Gándara & Ee, 2021). Trust is the bridge that transforms compliance into connection.

How?

Trust is built through deliberate, repeatable adult actions that protect dignity while fostering belonging. Classrooms become spaces of safety when educators intentionally design routines, language, and relationships with care and clarity.

1. Establish Clear Boundaries Around Confidentiality

Be explicit about what information is collected, who has access to it, and how it is used. Avoid unnecessary data requests that may expose immigration or residency status, and consistently reinforce inclusive language such as *"all students and families have the right to learn safely."*

2. Build Relational Rituals Into the School Day

Incorporate predictable routines such as daily check-ins, morning circles, or brief reflections that provide students with voice in low-risk ways. Consistency helps students associate routine with safety and belonging.

3. Use Asset-Based Language Consistently

Replace deficit narratives with affirming descriptions that recognize resilience, cultural knowledge, and community strengths. Language shapes mindset, and mindset shapes adult actions and expectations.

4. Engage Bilingual and Bicultural Staff Intentionally

Include paraprofessionals, office staff, custodians, and community liaisons in communication and professional learning. These adults often serve as trusted bridges for families and play a critical role in relationship-building.

5. Teach Allyship Explicitly

Use literature, discussion, and shared classroom norms to normalize empathy, fairness, and advocacy across migration experiences. When trust is paired with empowerment, fear begins to loosen its grip.

Reflection Prompts

- How do my daily interactions communicate safety, consistency, and care?
- Which classroom routines might unintentionally expose or isolate students from undocumented homes?
- How do we talk about confidentiality and cultural sensitivity as a staff?
- Whose trust have I earned, and whose trust still needs repair?

Then What?

Once trust is established, the next step is sustaining it through consistent systems. Individual acts of care matter, but alignment across classrooms and offices protects students over time. **Resource 4.1: Sample Family Rights Flyer** provides an example of how schools can clearly communicate legal rights in accessible, trust-building ways.

Schoolwide consistency reinforces trust. When family forms, translation services, and communication protocols align around confidentiality, families see that protection is not dependent on a single adult. When words about safety are matched by actions—how absences are handled or how staff respond to outside inquiries—trust becomes durable rather than fragile.

What If?

What if trust feels slow to build? That is expected. Families and students who have learned caution will test consistency before believing it. Stay steady and predictable. Schools across the country demonstrate that trust grows through small, repeated actions. When confidentiality becomes a shared commitment rather than a checkbox, students no longer feel forced to live two lives—one for home and one for school. They are free to be learners.

Way 14 — Building Bridges with Families Through Relational Safety

What?

For students from undocumented homes, the bridge between home and school can feel fragile—built on uncertainty and crossed with caution. Families often want to engage, yet fear of exposure or misunderstanding can make every interaction with school feel risky. Building relational safety means creating partnerships where families know their voice is valued, their privacy is respected, and their security will not be compromised.

Relational safety is not a program; it is a posture. It emerges through consistent empathy, discretion, and cultural humility— how names are pronounced, how translation is offered without prompting, and how every family is greeted with dignity regardless of documentation. When relational safety is present, families move from silent observers to active collaborators in their children's education.

Why?

Family engagement rests on trust, and for families from undocumented homes, trust must be demonstrated through action rather than promised through words. The National Immigration Law Center (2023) reports that many immigrant parents avoid school meetings, events, and even daily routines due to fear that their status could be revealed. A 2024 Urban Institute study found that forty-one percent of mixed-status families reduced contact with public institutions, including schools, amid heightened enforcement.

This distance impacts students. When families feel excluded or unsafe, communication gaps widen and academic and emotional supports weaken. Conversely, when educators build authentic, protective relationships, students show higher attendance, stronger motivation, and deeper belonging (Gándara & Ee, 2021). Relational safety shifts engagement from transactional tasks to shared purpose—moving from "sign this form" to "let's work together to help your child thrive."

How?

Relational safety is built through intentional, repeatable adult actions that protect dignity and invite partnership. When schools thoughtfully design how interactions occur, families are more likely to engage with trust rather than fear.

1. **Lead With Empathy Before Inquiry**

Begin conversations with care and curiosity rather than compliance-driven questioning. Avoid intrusive questions about origin, status, or processes, and keep dialogue centered on student growth, well-being, and aspirations.

2. **Communicate Through Trusted Channels**

Identify the platforms families already use—such as messaging apps, community liaisons, or established communication tools—and adopt them where appropriate. Respect boundaries by limiting unnecessary sharing of addresses, group information, or personal details.

3. **Establish Confidential Points of Contact**

Designate trained, bilingual staff who can support families with forms, transportation, or access to resources while upholding strict privacy protocols. Ensure this role is visible, consistent, and clearly communicated to families.

4. **Create Family Spaces That Feel Safe**

Design front offices and common areas to be welcoming rather than intimidating. Use clear messaging that affirms all families are welcome, provide translation services, and offer discreet assistance for completing documents that may cause fear or confusion.

5. Offer Optional Learning Opportunities on Rights and Resources

Partner with trusted community organizations to share information—such as student rights under *Plyler v. Doe*—in judgment-free settings. Participation should always be optional and framed as empowerment, not obligation. **Resource 4.2: Confidentiality Audit Checklist** supports schools in examining enrollment and communication practices through a lens of safety, dignity, and care.

Reflection Prompts

- How do our communication systems demonstrate respect for family confidentiality?
- When have we explicitly assured families that their information will not be shared without consent?
- Do our school events celebrate diversity in ways that protect families from undocumented homes?
- Who already holds trust with these families, and how can we amplify their role?

Then What?

Relational safety strengthens when it is institutional rather than individual. Schools that rely on a few trusted staff risk losing momentum with turnover. Embedding safety into policy, procedure, and professional learning ensures consistency across classrooms and offices.

Create clear communication guidelines that protect privacy and train all staff—teachers, office assistants, bus drivers, and custodians—to uphold them. Review forms, letters, and digital platforms for inclusive, non-threatening language. As partnerships with community organizations deepen, families come to see schools as allies rather than risks.

What If?

What if families remain hesitant to engage? Expect caution and remain steady. Trust develops through consistency over time, not urgency. Maintain predictable practices and honor boundaries. Relational safety turns schools into anchors of stability. When educators lead with compassion, confidentiality, and cultural responsiveness, families receive a clear message: you belong here, your child belongs here, and together we are stronger.

Way 15 — Protecting Privacy and Ensuring Equitable Access Through Policy and Systems

What?

Trust and relationships thrive at the classroom level—but if school or district systems are inconsistent, even the most compassionate teachers can't fully protect students from undocumented homes. Systemic trust demands structural integrity: policies, protocols, and data practices that guarantee confidentiality and equitable access for all students.

Protecting privacy is not just a moral responsibility—it's a legal one. *Plyler v. Doe* (1982) affirmed that all children, regardless of citizenship or immigration status, are entitled to a free public education. Yet across the country, inconsistent enrollment procedures, unclear documentation policies, and limited staff training have created unintended barriers that conflict with this right.

When schools adopt clear systems that prioritize privacy, eliminate unnecessary data collection, and align access across all departments, they create consistency that builds community-wide confidence. Systemic safeguards ensure that no child's opportunity depends on which office staff member happens to handle their form.

Why?

In the absence of clear policy, confusion breeds risk. Families often encounter mixed messages from schools about which documents are required for enrollment, verification, or extracurricular participation. A 2023 Migration Policy Institute report found that twenty-seven percent of immigrant families nationwide were asked for documents not legally required to enroll their children, such as Social Security numbers or proof of citizenship.

This inconsistency creates unnecessary barriers and deepens distrust. When families from undocumented homes sense potential exposure, they often withdraw from participation—opting out of lunch programs, tutoring, or transportation assistance for fear of being reported. The result is a silent inequity: students who most need access to resources are the least likely to use them.

Equitable systems also matter for staff. Without explicit guidance, educators may act out of good intent but limited understanding, inadvertently asking inappropriate questions or collecting information that places families at risk. Clear policy removes guesswork, ensures compliance, and reinforces the district's core value of inclusion.

How?

Protecting students from undocumented homes requires systems that are intentionally designed to safeguard privacy and ensure access. This work begins by examining how enrollment, data, and communication practices either reinforce trust—or unintentionally create barriers.

1. Review enrollment and documentation processes

Conduct a districtwide audit to identify which forms request personal data not required by law. Federal guidance explicitly prohibits schools from denying enrollment based on citizenship status or requiring Social Security numbers (U.S. Department of Education, 2023). Replace unnecessary fields with unique student identifiers or alternative verifications such as utility bills or community letters.

2. Establish clear confidentiality policies

Develop written protocols that specify who can access student information and under what circumstances. Include explicit guidance on how to respond if external agencies or law enforcement request student data. Provide annual training so all staff—front office, transportation, food services, and instructional—understand confidentiality laws and district procedures.

3. Align systems across departments

Ensure consistency between enrollment, nutrition services, counseling, and extracurricular programs. If one system contradicts another, families receive mixed signals. Alignment prevents inadvertent exposure and ensures equitable access.

4. Integrate privacy training into onboarding

Every new staff member—teachers, substitutes, coaches, and support staff—should receive explicit guidance on FERPA protections and district expectations related to students from undocumented homes. Annual refreshers keep policies active rather than buried in handbooks.

5. Provide multilingual and accessible information

Families must understand their rights in their primary language. Translate forms, signage, and communications related to privacy and access. Partner with trusted community organizations to host informational sessions where families can ask questions in safe, supportive environments.

6. Monitor and evaluate regularly

Establish a process for reviewing concerns related to data privacy or access barriers. When issues arise, treat them as opportunities to strengthen systems rather than assign blame.

Reflection Prompts

- Do our enrollment and registration processes collect only what is legally necessary?
- How do we communicate to families that their personal information is protected?
- Are all staff—including non-instructional roles—trained in privacy protocols?
- When was the last time our district reviewed how student data are stored, shared, and archived?

Then What?

Once privacy protocols are secure, leaders must ensure equitable access follows. Access includes extracurricular activities, mental health services, advanced coursework, and postsecondary planning. Policies should explicitly state that students from undocumented homes are eligible for all programs available to their peers.

Counselors and advisors can proactively remove barriers in scholarships, college applications, and dual-enrollment programs by offering alternatives to citizenship-based requirements and sharing local opportunities that do not require documentation. Many districts also adopt "safe zone" or "sensitive location" resolutions that clarify separation between schools and immigration enforcement. When families know these safeguards exist, trust deepens. Equity-focused systems extend beyond protection—they provide opportunity. **Resource 4.3: Community Partnership Mapping Template** supports schools in strengthening collaboration with trusted local organizations that can expand access without increasing risk.

What If?

What if every family entering a school office knew—without hesitation—that their personal information would never be used against them? What if students could access meals, transportation, technology, and enrichment without fear?

Imagine systems so aligned that every adult—from superintendent to substitute—understands how to protect privacy and ensure equity. In those schools, fear gives way to trust, and compliance gives way to belonging. That is *Plyler v. Doe* fully realized—not just in law, but in lived experience.

Way 16 — Partnering with Community Organizations for Advocacy and Family Empowerment

What?

Schools cannot shoulder the challenges faced by students from undocumented homes alone. True equity requires a web of partnerships that extend beyond school walls—collaborations with community organizations, faith-based groups, legal aid networks, and advocacy coalitions that share the mission of safety, stability, and empowerment.

Partnering with community organizations allows schools to move from providing short-term support to building long-term systems of care. These partnerships create resource bridges for families navigating housing insecurity, food access, healthcare, and legal uncertainty. They also empower students and caregivers to become advocates for themselves and their communities.

The goal is not charity—it's collaboration. When schools and community organizations align around trust and advocacy, families gain both the knowledge and the confidence to navigate systems that were not built with them in mind.

Why?

Community partnerships strengthen the educational ecosystem by multiplying the reach of resources. According to the Urban Institute (2023), students in mixed-status families are 37% more likely to experience housing instability and twice as likely to lack access to healthcare. Schools alone cannot meet all these needs—but partnerships can.

When schools connect families to trusted community organizations, they build a circle of stability that reinforces learning. The National Center for Community Schools (2024) found that schools with strong community partnerships saw a 22% increase in family engagement and a 15% improvement in student attendance, particularly among students from undocumented homes.

Partnerships also provide schools with expertise. Legal service agencies, immigrant rights groups, and cultural organizations can guide staff on how to communicate about sensitive issues, protect family privacy, and navigate policy shifts. This collaborative expertise allows educators to focus on their primary mission—teaching—while ensuring families receive accurate, culturally informed support.

How?

1. Map your local ecosystem

Start by identifying existing community organizations that serve immigrant or multilingual populations. Create a partnership map that includes nonprofits, advocacy networks, cultural centers, and faith communities. Note which services they provide—legal aid, translation, food distribution, counseling—and identify potential overlaps or gaps. To make safety visible, **Resource 4.4: Safe Zone Poster Template** communicates belonging and confidentiality.

Resource 4.4: Safe Zone Poster Elements

Poster Element	Sample Language	Customization Notes
Affirmation Statement	This is a safe and welcoming learning space for every student.	Adjust language to reflect district commitments and tone.
Rights Reminder	All students have the right to attend school regardless of immigration status.	Align with Resource 4.1 language where appropriate.
Confidentiality Message	Your personal information is respected and protected.	Ensure consistency with confidentiality policies.
Support Signal	If you need help or have questions, trusted adults are here to support you.	List roles or locations rather than individual names if preferred.

2. Build relationships before crises

Partnerships built on urgency often fade once the crisis ends. Begin outreach proactively. Invite organizational representatives to meet with school leadership, attend cultural nights, or co-host community resource fairs. Building rapport before families need help ensures smoother collaboration when support is required.

3. Develop memoranda of understanding (MOUs)

Formal agreements clarify boundaries, responsibilities, and confidentiality expectations. MOUs protect families and the school by outlining how data is shared (if at all), how referrals are handled, and how both parties communicate about cases.

4. Offer space, not just support

Schools can serve as community hubs by hosting evening workshops, citizenship information sessions, or language classes provided by external organizations. Making the school a trusted meeting space strengthens its identity as a community partner rather than merely an institution.

5. Celebrate partnership wins publicly

When partnerships make a tangible difference—a student gains legal protection through a pro bono clinic or a family secures stable housing—celebrate those successes collectively. Public acknowledgment builds community trust and encourages others to seek support.

6. Include students and families as co-designers

Invite families and older students to share what resources are most needed. When they help shape partnerships, the resulting programs reflect authentic priorities rather than assumptions. To ensure clarity and consistency, **Resource 4.5: Family Communication Guide** supports culturally responsive messaging.

Reflection Prompts

- Which community organizations currently serve our families, and how are we partnering with them?
- Are our partnerships grounded in reciprocity, or do they rely on one-way support?
- How do we communicate the availability of community resources to families safely and respectfully?
- What might families teach us about which partnerships they trust most?

Then What?

To align adult practice with family trust, **Resource 4.6: Professional Learning Agenda** supports staff learning. It is critical to offer professional learning to staff to help build trust. Once trust is solidified, educators build strong partnerships. When strong partnerships exist, schools can take the next step: advocacy. Advocacy means using our collective influence to remove systemic barriers and expand access at the local and state levels.

Educators can advocate by:

+ Providing testimony about the educational needs of undocumented families at school board or city council meetings.
+ Partnering with legal experts to inform district policy revisions.
+ Sharing aggregated, anonymous data about barriers families face to drive equitable policy reform.

At the same time, schools should nurture advocacy among families. Host workshops that help caregivers understand their educational rights and empower older students to engage civically without fear. Provide materials on how to contact local representatives or participate in school advisory councils safely and effectively. When advocacy becomes a shared endeavor, schools shift from being service providers to agents of structural change.

What If?

What if every community surrounding a school viewed undocumented students not as invisible, but as indispensable? What if legal clinics, libraries, cultural centers, and schools operated as one interconnected support system—sharing resources, honoring privacy, and celebrating resilience?

In this vision, partnerships transform the educational experience from survival to empowerment. Families no longer navigate systems alone; they walk alongside allies. Students grow up seeing adults working collectively for justice, not merely compliance.

When schools lead through partnership, they signal to families: *You are not alone here. We see you. We stand with you.* Together, communities can replace isolation with inclusion, fear with advocacy, and silence with solidarity.

Closing Reflection

On the last day of school, Marisol stood at her locker, the edges of that unsigned permission slip still tucked between her notebooks. Her teacher stopped by, smiling gently. "You know, I saved you a script from the play," she said, handing it over. "You would've made a great lead."

Marisol smiled, unsure what to say. She knew the year had changed her—not because of the play she missed, but because of what her teacher and counselor had done afterward. They'd found ways to reach her family without paperwork or fear—sending messages through trusted community liaisons, hosting student showcases that didn't require forms, and visiting homes just to listen.

By spring, her mother, Lucía, had volunteered to help in the cafeteria. "Here, I feel safe," she told the counselor one afternoon, her voice steady for the first time.

That summer, when Marisol auditioned for the next school play, she handed in her signed form without hesitation. It wasn't the absence of fear that changed her—it was the presence of trust.

When educators see every student through the lens of possibility rather than paperwork, we help them rediscover their courage to be seen.

The Constellation of Learning™ Synopsis

 The theme of **Transformational & Adaptive Leadership** anchors this chapter, urging educators to lead courageously for students from undocumented homes. Adaptive leadership demands that we confront fear, uncertainty, and policy barriers with empathy and informed advocacy. Transformational change begins when we ensure students know that their stories are protected and their dreams are valid.

Leadership under this constellation is not about compliance—it's about conviction. When educators learn students' realities and amplify their voices, schools evolve from institutions of regulation to havens of belonging. Adaptive leaders adjust systems to human lives rather than expecting human lives to conform to systems.

Hallway Confessions – Daily Practice and Perspective

One morning, a teacher with whom Danny worked shared quietly in the staff lounge: "I've been keeping an extra lunch in my fridge—just in case one of my students forgets theirs. She never says she's hungry, but I can tell."

That same week, a custodian mentioned that he'd walked a student home who was afraid to be seen near the school gates after pickup time. Neither gesture made it into a policy memo, yet both transformed the climate of care.

In every school, quiet acts of protection happen daily—teachers choosing neutral language on forms, counselors discreetly connecting families to services, office staff translating newsletters by hand when no interpreter is available.

These unheralded choices matter. They communicate that inclusion isn't an initiative—it's a moral instinct. Each small act, layered together, builds an invisible network of compassion that keeps fear at bay.

The next time you pass a family in the hallway who hesitates before asking for help, remember: your presence, tone, and trust may be the bridge they've been waiting for.

Leadership is not measured only by visibility or authority, but by what—and who—it chooses to protect when the stakes are high. The most consequential leadership moments often happen quietly, when adults decide whether student stories will be honored or erased. Leadership that changes lives begins with the bravery to protect stories that were never meant to be silenced.

Leadership that changes lives begins with the bravery to protect stories that were never meant to be silenced.

The Dismissal Bell – The Five A's

When the final bell rings, some students leave school carrying relief—and others carry fear about what comes next. For students from undocumented homes, learning is inseparable from trust. Safety is not a feeling; it is a condition created by adult choices, policies, and daily practices. When schools protect confidentiality, communicate with care, and partner with families without suspicion, they become places of refuge rather than risk. Advocacy begins long before a crisis arises— it lives in the systems we design to ensure that every student can learn without fear of exposure. When trust is protected, belonging follows, and education becomes the shield it was meant to be.

Action Step	Description
Audit	Examine every system, form, and process for language or practices that may deter undocumented families.
Adjust	Replace deficit-based assumptions with inclusive, asset-based language.
Advocate	Speak up at school board meetings, in staff discussions, and in policy forums to defend the educational rights of all children.
Assemble	Partner with organizations that can amplify school-based impact into community-wide advocacy.
Attitude Ask	Commit to asking yourself daily: *Am I leading from fear or from empathy?*

Black Students: Honoring Identity, Driving Equity, and Raising Expectations

Opening Vignette

Jaylen had a rhythm for everything—his step into the classroom, the way he spun his pencil between his fingers, even how he tapped the beat of his favorite Kendrick Lamar song against the side of his desk. When he raised his hand, he did it with purpose. But when the teacher called on someone else—again—his arm dropped slowly. The rhythm broke.

He didn't know it, but every teacher in that middle school had heard his name more than once in the staff lounge. "He's smart, just needs to focus." "He's got leadership potential, but he can be a handful." Jaylen had learned to read tone as fluently as text. When the assistant principal walked past him in the hallway, Jaylen's smile faded into neutrality; blending in felt safer than standing out.

One afternoon, his English teacher asked the class to analyze a Langston Hughes poem. Jaylen leaned forward, words forming quietly in his mind. But before he could speak, another student offered an answer—and the discussion moved on. After class, Jaylen stayed behind and said softly, "You never call on me anymore." The teacher paused, realizing too late how invisible she had made him feel.

The next day, she asked him to lead the discussion. Jaylen's rhythm returned, but it wasn't just the beat of confidence—it was the sound of being seen.

Framing the Challenge

Across the United States, Black students continue to face persistent inequities that reflect both systemic and interpersonal bias. According to the 2023 *Condition of Education* report from the National Center for Education Statistics, Black students represent roughly 15% of the nation's public-school population but account for 38% of all out-of-school suspensions. Meanwhile, enrollment in advanced coursework and gifted programs remains disproportionately low. Only 9% of students enrolled in Advanced Placement courses nationwide identify as Black, compared to 48% who identify as white (U.S. Department of Education, 2023).

The data reveal not a deficit in ability, but a pattern of exclusion—rooted in bias, expectations, and institutional habit. Researchers have long found that teacher expectations can powerfully shape student outcomes. Rosenthal and Jacobson's foundational "Pygmalion effect" work, replicated across decades, demonstrates that when teachers expect success, students tend to achieve it. Conversely, when low expectations persist, they quietly lower the ceiling for student growth.

Culturally responsive teaching scholar Gloria Ladson-Billings (2021) reminds us that schools were never designed with equity as their organizing principle—they were designed for assimilation. Thus, educators must actively reconstruct systems that affirm identity rather than neutralize it. Black students deserve learning spaces where their culture, language, and history are recognized not as enrichment topics, but as essential knowledge.

The last few years have added both urgency and complexity. Following the national reckoning on race in 2020, districts adopted diversity statements and equity frameworks. Yet, many teachers still express uncertainty about "how" to translate equity from principle into practice. Some fear saying the wrong thing; others fear confronting their own bias. The result is often paralysis masked as politeness.

Meanwhile, students like Jaylen feel the gap between what schools promise and what they experience. For many Black students, microaggressions accumulate—a mispronounced name, a comment about "talking too loud," a lowered grade for "attitude." Each moment chips away at belonging. When Black students feel disconnected from their school identity, academic engagement declines, and trust with adults fractures.

Addressing this challenge requires not just awareness, but deliberate, daily acts of change. The work begins with expectation—what we believe our students are capable of—and continues through curriculum, relationships, and leadership. The following strategies focus on rebuilding the foundation of expectation that determines whether Black students see themselves reflected in the story of school success.

Too often, culture is treated as something separate from instruction—something to address when time allows rather than something that shapes every learning moment. When we understand culture as the soil in which learning grows, connection becomes the pathway to rigor. When culture leads the lesson, connection leads the learning.

When we understand culture as the soil in which learning grows, connection becomes the pathway to rigor. When culture leads the lesson, connection leads the learning.

Way 17: Recognize and Rebuild Expectations

What?

Equity starts in the mind before it ever reaches the lesson plan. To support Black students fully, we must confront implicit bias and rebuild the expectations we hold for academic success, behavior, and belonging. Expectations are the invisible architecture of school culture. They show up in the tone we use, the patience we extend, the feedback we give, and the opportunities we offer—or withhold.

When adult belief systems default to deficit narratives, students feel it. A raised eyebrow, a quicker referral, a "not ready" placement, or praise that stays surface-level all send messages about what we think is possible. Rebuilding expectations means shifting from assumptions about what students lack to disciplined recognition of what Black students bring: brilliance, insight, leadership, humor, persistence, and deep relational awareness. This Way is not about adopting a slogan. It is about changing daily adult decisions so our belief becomes visible and consistent.

Why?

Bias—both implicit and systemic—has measurable impact. The Stanford Center for Education Policy Analysis (2022) found that Black students were more likely to receive lower teacher evaluations than white peers with identical work quality. That matters because evaluations often influence everything that follows: who gets nudged toward advanced coursework, who gets labeled "unmotivated," who is referred for behavior, and who is described as "college material." When bias goes unexamined, it doesn't stay private. It becomes policy in practice.

The good news is that patterns can change when adults choose to change them. In Chicago Public Schools, anti-bias professional learning paired with restorative discipline led to a twenty percent decrease in exclusionary discipline for Black students and higher student-reported trust in teachers (University of Chicago Consortium, 2023). That outcome reinforces what we see in schools: when students feel seen, challenged, and supported—at the same time—they take more risks, engage more deeply, and persist longer. Rebuilding expectations is not extra work. It is foundational work that protects Black students from lowered opportunity and makes rigor feel real rather than selective.

How?

Rebuilding expectations requires intentional adult moves that show up in data, language, and daily interactions. This is not about perfection or performing equity. It is about creating consistent conditions where Black students experience belief as a lived reality, not a stated value.

1. Run an expectation audit that names patterns, not people

Use grades, referrals, advanced-course enrollment, and participation data to surface where opportunity is uneven. Look for patterns such as Black students clustered in lower groups, called on less often, or underrepresented in leadership. Discuss findings as design problems the adults own, not student problems to explain away.

2. Practice "pause and pivot" in the moment of reaction

When you feel yourself labeling behavior quickly, pause and ask, "What is this student communicating, and what support is missing?" Replace "defiant" with a question that invites understanding and a response that preserves dignity. This shift changes how consequences are applied and how relationships are repaired.

3. Pair high expectations with visible, predictable support

Rigor is not more work; it is meaningful challenge with scaffolds that help students succeed. Plan supports up front—models, exemplars, sentence frames, re-teaching cycles, and clear success criteria—so belief is built into instruction, not offered only after students struggle. Make feedback specific and forward-moving so students can see the path, not just the grade.

4. Use student voice to check your reality, not your intention

Build consistent ways to hear how Black students experience fairness, challenge, and belonging—surveys, focus groups, and quick one-on-one "minute meetings." Ask what feels supportive, what feels biased, and what feels inconsistent across classrooms. Treat student perception as evidence that helps adults adjust design and practice.

Reflection Prompts

+ Where in my classroom or school do Black students experience lowered access, softer expectations, or quicker consequences?
+ When I feel myself reacting fast to behavior, what assumptions am I making—and what would it look like to "pause and pivot"?
+ How do I define rigor in practice, and do Black students consistently receive both challenge and support in my room?

Then What?

After awareness comes disciplined follow-through. Build expectation check-ins into team time and PLC agendas, and name one specific adult practice you are changing this month—feedback language, grouping decisions, referral thresholds, participation routines, or access to advanced tasks. Track small indicators early: more equitable calling patterns, fewer subjective referrals, stronger completion rates on complex tasks, and student comments that reflect increased trust.

To move from data collection to meaningful action, **Resource 5.1: Equity Data Tracker** supports teams in identifying patterns that require reflection and response. When teams use that tool consistently, expectation work becomes schoolwide rather than teacher-by-teacher. Over time, the culture shifts: belief becomes more consistent across classrooms, advanced opportunities become less gatekept, discipline becomes less predictable by race, and Black students experience school as a place where excellence is assumed and supported.

What If?

What if staff feel defensive when expectations and bias are named? That response is common because no one wants to believe they are part of harm. Start by grounding the conversation in patterns and systems, not character, and remind the team that this is about improving design, not assigning blame.

What if you worry that raising expectations will increase frustration or pushback from students? High expectations without support will do that—so don't separate them. Lead with clarity, scaffolds, and consistent feedback that communicates belief: "This is challenging because it matters, and we will get there together." When adults rebuild expectations with support and consistency, Black students don't have to fight to be seen as capable. They can focus on learning.

Way 18: Center Culture as Curriculum

What?

Curriculum always tells a story about who matters, whose knowledge counts, and what excellence looks like. When instruction reflects only a narrow slice of the human experience, students learn—often silently—who belongs in the story of learning and who does not. Centering culture as curriculum means intentionally designing learning so that Black history, excellence, innovation, and identity are embedded across subjects and grade levels.

This is not an add-on unit or a celebratory moment reserved for February. It is a through-line. When Black students see their culture reflected consistently and rigorously, curriculum becomes a mirror as well as a window. Learning shifts from compliance to connection because students recognize themselves as contributors to knowledge, not outsiders to it.

Why?

Representation shapes both cognition and motivation. Research on culturally responsive teaching shows that when students see themselves reflected in texts, examples, and leadership narratives, engagement increases and self-efficacy strengthens (Hammond, 2020). Conversely, when Black students rarely encounter affirming representations, they may internalize the message that success requires distancing themselves from their identity.

Curriculum audits conducted across multiple states reveal persistent gaps. EdTrust (2023) found that fewer than twenty percent of secondary English reading lists include a Black author, and many social studies courses reduce Black history primarily to enslavement and the civil rights movement—omitting centuries of intellectual, artistic, scientific, and civic leadership. Gloria Ladson-Billings (2021) reminds us that culturally relevant pedagogy is not about lowering standards; it is about grounding rigor in relevance. Rigor disconnected from identity may produce compliance, but it rarely produces curiosity, persistence, or joy in learning.

How?

Centering culture as curriculum requires intentional planning and collective responsibility. These steps focus on redesigning instruction so representation is sustained rather than symbolic.

1. Audit the storyline of your curriculum

Review anchor texts, instructional materials, visuals, and examples across units. Ask whose voices are centered and whose are absent. Replace isolated or token references with sustained inclusion so Black perspectives appear as integral, not exceptional.

2. Integrate culture across disciplines, not just humanities

Highlight Black excellence in science, mathematics, technology, and the arts as part of core instruction. Normalizing contributions from figures such as Mae Jemison, George Washington Carver, and Dr. Kizzmekia Corbett reinforces that brilliance is expected, not surprising.

3. Leverage community expertise as academic capital

Invite local historians, artists, entrepreneurs, or scholars to co-teach lessons or consult on units. When students see knowledge embodied within their community, learning feels both credible and connected.

4. Teach students to create and critique narratives

Provide opportunities for students to analyze media portrayals of Black identity and develop counter-narratives through writing, discussion, podcasts, or art. This builds critical thinking while affirming voice and agency.

5. Measure belonging as a learning outcome

Incorporate questions such as "I see my culture represented in what we learn" into surveys and reflections. Treat belonging as essential data that informs instructional design, not as a secondary sentiment. Embedded directly into instructional planning, **Resource**

5.2. Culturally Responsive Unit Planner supports educators in aligning identity, rigor, and relevance within daily learning.

Reflection Prompts
- How consistently does my curriculum reflect Black voices, perspectives, and contributions?
- Where might representation be present in name but shallow in substance?
- Do my instructional choices affirm identity as central to rigor or treat it as enrichment?

Then What?

Begin collaboratively. Work with grade-level or content teams to redesign one unit each semester through an equity lens. Identify where representation deepens conceptual understanding rather than merely adding content. Track changes in engagement, participation, and quality of student work to understand the instructional impact.

As teams share redesigned units and student outcomes, culturally centered curriculum becomes normalized rather than exceptional. Over time, students experience learning spaces where their culture is not something to be explained or defended—it is assumed, respected, and built upon.

What If?

What if students encountered Black protagonists as scientists, innovators, leaders, and everyday learners across the school year? What if the curriculum told the story of possibility rather than limitation?

When culture is centered as curriculum, Black students no longer have to search for themselves in the margins of learning. They see their identities reflected in the work of knowing and creating.

And when students recognize themselves as part of the story, engagement deepens, confidence grows, and learning becomes personal as well as rigorous.

Way 19: Redefine Discipline Through Dignity

What?

Discipline systems communicate values long before they enforce rules. When schools prioritize control over connection, discipline becomes a mechanism for compliance rather than a pathway to growth. For many Black students, this dynamic results in disproportionate surveillance of normal adolescent behavior and quicker escalation to punitive responses.

Redefining discipline through dignity means shifting from punishment to repair. It centers relationships, accountability, and belonging rather than exclusion. Discipline becomes an opportunity to teach, restore, and reconnect—without stripping students of their humanity or access to learning.

Why?

National data shows persistent inequities. Black students are suspended nearly four times more often than their white peers for similar behaviors (U.S. Department of Education Office for Civil Rights, 2023). Research by Gregory et al. (2022) links these disparities to implicit bias in how behaviors such as "defiance," "attitude," or "non-compliance" are interpreted. Each removal from class represents lost instructional time and reinforces the message that belonging is conditional.

Schools that adopt restorative approaches see different outcomes. In Oakland Unified School District, suspension rates for Black students dropped by fifty-six percent over five years following the implementation of restorative circles and staff bias training

(Oakland USD Equity Report, 2023). These shifts did not reduce expectations. They clarified them. When discipline preserves dignity, students are more likely to remain engaged, accountable, and connected to school.

How?

Redefining discipline requires coordinated adult practice and system-level consistency. These steps focus on changing how schools respond to conflict rather than who they remove.

1. **Shift the goal from control to connection**

Reframe "classroom management" as relationship management. Co-create norms with students and revisit them regularly so expectations feel shared rather than imposed.

2. **Use restorative conversations before consequences**

Train staff to ask, "Who was affected?" and "What needs to happen to make it right?" before assigning punitive measures. This approach centers accountability while preserving dignity.

3. **Analyze discipline data monthly for patterns**

Disaggregate referrals and consequences by race and gender. When disparities appear, treat them as system signals that require adult reflection and adjustment rather than student correction.

4. **Create structures for student-led repair**

Establish peer justice teams or mediation groups to resolve low-level conflicts. These structures build empathy, leadership, and ownership while reducing escalation.

5. **Coach response language intentionally**

Support teachers in shifting from compliance-driven language to collaborative language. Phrases like "Let's figure this out together" communicate accountability without humiliation. When conflict arises, **Resource 5.3: Dignity-Centered Restorative Framework** supports responses that strengthen relationships while maintaining clear expectations.

Reflection Prompts
- When was the last time I repaired harm with a student rather than issuing a consequence?
- How do my responses to conflict vary depending on who initiates the conflict?
- Does my classroom culture rely on fear of consequences or mutual respect?

Then What?

Protect time for restoration. Build restorative conversations, circles, or mediation into the master schedule and treat them as instructional time rather than interruptions. When repair is routine instead of reactive, students learn that mistakes do not exile them from the community.

As dignity-centered discipline becomes consistent, referral patterns shift, relationships deepen, and classrooms stabilize. Over time, students internalize that accountability is a path back into belonging, not a door out of it.

What If?

What if discipline meetings began with listening rather than referrals? What if students believed correction was an invitation to grow instead of a signal to leave? Redefining discipline does not mean removing accountability. It means humanizing it. Dignity and order are not opposites—they are partners. When discipline protects dignity, Black students experience school as a place that corrects with care and holds them to high expectations without exclusion.

Way 20 — Elevate Black Joy and Leadership

What?

Black joy is both resistance and renewal. In schools, elevating Black joy is more than celebration—it is a pedagogical choice that nurtures resilience, creativity, and hope. When Black students experience joy in learning and leadership, they begin to rewrite internal narratives about who they are and what is possible for them.

Too often, school narratives focus on struggle, gaps, and correction. This Way intentionally shifts the lens toward brilliance, possibility, and leadership. Elevating Black joy affirms that excellence is not exceptional—it is expected. Joy becomes a visible, sustaining force that strengthens belonging and fuels engagement.

Why?

Conversations about Black students frequently center on deficit language—achievement gaps, discipline data, and trauma. While acknowledging barriers matter, constant exposure to deficit framing can erode self-perception and narrow how educators and students alike define success.

Research on positive racial identity demonstrates the power of affirmation. Nasir and Snyder (2022) found that when students experience affirmation of cultural pride and identity, academic engagement increases and discipline referrals decrease. Joy builds stamina for hard learning. It reminds students that school is not only a place to endure, but a place to thrive.

Schools that intentionally elevate joy also see cultural benefits. Staff morale improves, relationships deepen, and leadership becomes distributed rather than gatekept. When joy is visible, it signals that Black students are valued not only for resilience, but for creativity, leadership, and contribution.

How?

Elevating joy and leadership requires consistent adult action and intentional structures. These steps focus on making joy visible, sustained, and connected to leadership.

1. **Highlight Black excellence year-round**

Celebrate achievements in academics, arts, STEM, leadership, and athletics throughout the school year. Use hallway displays, announcements, and school communications to normalize excellence rather than confining recognition to heritage months.

2. **Build mentorship pipelines that develop leadership**

Pair younger students with older peers, alumni, or community mentors who model success and advocacy. Programs such as My Brother's Keeper demonstrate gains in GPA and attendance when mentorship is consistent and relational (Obama Foundation, 2023).

3. **Celebrate culture through student-led experiences**

Support events such as spoken-word showcases, step performances, or Afro-futurism art exhibitions that center creativity and voice. When students plan and lead these spaces, they practice leadership grounded in identity.

4. **Infuse joy into daily instruction**

Joy does not mean lowering rigor. It means emotionally engaging learning through music, movement, humor, affirmation, and culturally affirming examples. Engagement deepens when students feel seen and energized.

5. **Elevate leadership through service and advocacy**

Support Black student organizations and service projects that address local issues. Position students as problem-solvers and change agents rather than passive participants.

Reflection Prompts

- How often do I intentionally highlight Black joy, creativity, and innovation in my classroom narrative?
- Do I publicly recognize excellence beyond grades and compliance?
- In what ways do I communicate that leadership is an identity, not just a position?

Then What?

Make joy visible at the system level. Create an annual opportunity—such as a Joy and Justice Week—that highlights Black student work across disciplines and leadership roles. Invite families, alumni, and community partners to participate so celebration extends beyond the classroom.

To support implementation, **Resource 5.4: Student Joy & Leadership Celebration Toolkit** helps schools intentionally recognize brilliance, leadership, and joy. **Resource 5.5: Family Voice & Partnership Spotlight Guide** elevates family voice as a strength within the school community. When joy is planned for, it becomes sustainable rather than sporadic.

What If?

What if joy were a standard in every school improvement plan? What if celebration consistently reflected students back to themselves as capable, creative, and worthy?

Joy transforms climate in ways data alone cannot capture. It restores rhythm to learning and reminds students that their voices matter. When schools elevate Black joy and leadership, they create spaces where students are not only supported—but celebrated.

Maya and Avery were not just navigating fifth grade—they were navigating school as Black girls in spaces where belonging was conditional. Their mother named what our data never did:

the daily microaggressions, the unchecked comments, and the ways discipline and peer interactions felt uneven and unsafe. These moments rarely appeared in formal reports, but they shaped how the twins moved through the building every single day.

As educators, we often celebrate equity in theory while missing it in practice. Maya and Avery taught me that being present in a school is not the same as being protected by it. Until schools are willing to listen when Black families say, *"This does not feel safe,"* we will continue confusing good intentions with just outcomes—and calling that equity.

So we stopped assuming and started listening.

We examined our school culture more honestly, asked hard questions about why bullying was occurring, and created space for student focus groups. Then we did something deceptively simple but profoundly important: we asked the students, "What should we do?"

They didn't hold back. And I'm glad they didn't.

They told us what adults had missed. They named patterns we had normalized. And in doing so, they shifted the work from adult-driven solutions to student-informed action. The message they received was clear: their voice mattered. They were heard. And we cared enough to act.

We implemented their ideas—and something powerful happened.

It worked.

Closing Reflection

Jaylen's rhythm carried him through eighth grade, but the song changed in high school. A new environment, new teachers, and unfamiliar expectations brought back that old hesitation. In freshman English, the teacher began each unit with a quote from Black authors—Baldwin, Angelou, Reynolds—and invited students to connect it to their lives. When Jaylen offered an interpretation, she didn't just nod; she asked him to elaborate. His peers listened. For the first time, he wasn't the exception—he was the example.

What made the difference wasn't one curriculum unit or an equity plan—it was belief, repeated daily, in a thousand ordinary moments. His teachers expected him to succeed, and he believed them. His principal made sure discipline policies protected dignity. His peers saw his leadership as natural, not novel.

The lesson for educators is clear: progress isn't a single initiative—it's the accumulation of consistent, human decisions that center care, culture, and high expectations. When we rebuild systems around those truths, we transform not just outcomes, but experiences.

The Constellation of Learning™ Synopsis

This chapter orbits **Student-Centered Culture & Engagement**, reminding us that celebrating Black excellence is an act of justice. Engagement begins when culture is not an afterthought but the heartbeat of learning. Representation, relevance, and relationship work together to ensure that every Black student sees their brilliance mirrored back in curriculum, leadership, and community.

This constellation challenges educators to create classrooms that don't simply *include* culture—they *are* culture. By inviting joy, pride, and identity into the learning process, we rewrite the narrative from underachievement to undeniable excellence. When we engage through empowerment, achievement becomes the natural rhythm of belonging.

Hallway Confessions – Daily Practice and Perspective

Some lessons about equity begin in the quiet corners of a hallway. A teacher once told us about a moment when she overheard two students teasing another for "talking too proper." Instead of ignoring it, she stopped, laughed with them softly, and said, "Funny—you sound like scholars. That's what smart sounds like." The laughter turned to smiles.

These small, unscripted interactions build belonging. The hallway smile after a tough class, the quick fist-bump before a test, the teacher who learns every student's playlist—these are equity moves, too. They cost nothing and change everything.

When we model vulnerability, admit mistakes, and show genuine curiosity about culture, students see that equity isn't a slogan—it's relationship in motion.

The Dismissal Bell – The Five A's

When the final bell rings, we must ask whether Black students leave our schools affirmed or merely managed. Too often, they spend the day navigating lowered expectations, disproportionate discipline, or curricula that overlook their brilliance and joy. These outcomes are not accidental—they are shaped by systems, beliefs, and daily decisions. When educators intentionally affirm identity, protect dignity, and design learning that centers on excellence rather than deficit, schools become places where Black students are free to thrive, not just comply. Equity is realized when joy, opportunity, and high expectations are not exceptions—but the norm.

Action Step	Description
Audit	Examine discipline, grading, and participation data for racial patterns. Pair numbers with student voice interviews.
Adjust	Revise curriculum maps, policies, and daily language to center cultural relevance and dignity.
Advocate	Use your influence to challenge inequitable structures—recommendations, honors placement, suspension thresholds.
Assemble	Form cross-role equity teams of students, teachers, and families to monitor progress and celebrate success.
Attitude Ask	How often do I equate "quiet" with "good"? How do my reactions reveal what I truly believe about Black brilliance? What would change tomorrow if I assumed every student is already extraordinary?

CHAPTER 6

Hispanic Students: Culture as Catalyst for Connection

Opening Vignette

Miguel, a ninth-grader at Riverside High, balances responsibilities at home and school. At home, he helps care for his younger siblings while his parents work long shifts. At school, he navigates English-only instruction while honoring his family's cultural heritage and language. One afternoon, Miguel struggles with a complex math problem. Instead of giving the answer, his teacher asks, "How would you explain this in your own words?" Miguel pauses, shares the solution first in Spanish, then in English. His teacher smiles—not just at the correct answer, but at the bridge he's building between two worlds.

For many students, the greatest barrier to learning is not ability, but distance—distance created when instruction feels unfamiliar, inaccessible, or disconnected from who they are. Language, when honored and leveraged, becomes one of the most powerful tools for connection. When we teach in the language of a student's heart, learning becomes a bridge instead of a barrier.

This story illustrates the dual pressures Hispanic students often face: academic expectations alongside cultural, linguistic, and familial responsibilities. Understanding these dynamics is essential for school leaders who strive to create equitable learning opportunities.

> When we teach in the language of a student's heart, learning becomes a bridge instead of a barrier.

Framing the Challenge

Hispanic students are the fastest-growing demographic in U.S. public schools, comprising 27% of the K–12 population in 2023 (NCES, 2023). Among English Learners (ELs), 75% are Hispanic, highlighting the critical need for targeted language and academic supports (NCES, 2023).

While enrollment is increasing, achievement gaps persist. The national graduation rate for Hispanic students is 81%, compared with 89% for White students (U.S. Dept. of Education, 2022). Chronic absenteeism is 12%, often influenced by socioeconomic factors such as parent work schedules, health barriers, or housing instability. Additionally, 53% of Hispanic students live in poverty, which impacts access to technology, tutoring, and enrichment opportunities (NCES, 2023).

These data demonstrate systemic inequities but also reveal opportunities. Schools that intentionally integrate culturally responsive instruction, bilingual supports, and family engagement can foster stronger outcomes. Leadership that validates identity and builds home-school-community partnerships creates the conditions for Hispanic students to thrive.

Key Takeaways:

- Hispanic students may require scaffolded language and academic supports.
- Socioeconomic pressures impact attendance, engagement, and access to resources.
- Leadership and instructional strategies that honor identity can bridge gaps and improve outcomes.

Table 6.1: Hispanic students data trends

Metric	National % / Data Source	Notes
Hispanic Student Enrollment	27% (NCES, 2023)	Largest growing group
English Learners (ELs)	75% (NCES, 2023)	Requires targeted supports
Graduation Rate	81% (U.S. Dept. of Education, 2022)	Gap vs. White students (89%)
Chronic Absenteeism	12% (ED, 2022)	Higher than national average (10%)
Students in Poverty	53% (NCES, 2023)	Impacts resources and academic support

Way 21 — Culturally Relevant Instruction

What?

This Way centers culturally relevant instruction as a design responsibility, not an add-on or accommodation. For Hispanic students, learning is most powerful when instruction intentionally reflects students' language, culture, histories, and lived experiences as assets rather than background context. Culturally relevant instruction moves beyond surface-level representation to affirm identity, elevate voice, and connect academic learning to the realities students navigate every day.

This work is not about "adding culture" to lessons after the fact. It is about planning with students in mind from the beginning—selecting texts, examples, tasks, and discussion structures that acknowledge bilingualism, family influence, community knowledge, and cultural values such as collectivism and perseverance. When educators design instruction that honors who students are, engagement deepens and rigor becomes more accessible rather than intimidating.

Why?

Students are more likely to engage when they see themselves reflected in what and how they are learning. Gloria Ladson-Billings and Geneva Gay have long emphasized that culturally relevant and culturally responsive teaching strengthens motivation, academic identity, and achievement by positioning students' cultures as sources of strength rather than obstacles. Gay's work, in particular, highlights that culturally responsive teaching improves both engagement and outcomes by making learning meaningful and affirming (Gay, 2018).

For many Hispanic students, disconnection from curriculum can quietly reinforce the message that academic success requires cultural separation or assimilation. When instruction ignores students' linguistic assets, family narratives, or cultural histories, students may comply without fully engaging—or disengage altogether. Culturally relevant instruction interrupts this pattern. It communicates that high expectations and cultural affirmation are not competing priorities. When students feel known and respected, they are more willing to participate, take risks, and persist through challenges.

How?

Culturally relevant instruction requires intentional planning and consistent adult action. These steps focus on instructional design choices educators control, not on asking students to adapt to systems that were not built with them in mind.

1. Design with cultural relevance in mind from the start

Begin lesson planning by identifying where students' cultural experiences, language, or community knowledge can naturally connect to the learning goal. This might include examples, scenarios, or applications that reflect students' lived realities rather than abstract or unfamiliar contexts.

2. Leverage bilingualism as an instructional strength

Use bilingual texts, visuals, and discussion supports to reinforce that language is an asset, not a barrier. When appropriate, allow students to process ideas in both languages, recognizing that deeper thinking often occurs when students can access their full linguistic repertoire.

3. Select texts and materials that reflect identity and history

Choose resources that include Hispanic authors, perspectives, and historical narratives beyond celebratory moments. Representation should be accurate, complex, and integrated into core instruction—not reserved for special occasions.

4. Structure learning to elevate student voice and experience

Build opportunities for students to share insights, stories, and perspectives through discussion, writing, or projects. Student voice should inform learning, not serve as an optional extension. When students' experiences are valued, participation becomes more authentic.

Reflection Prompts

- Where in our curriculum do Hispanic students see their language, culture, and histories reflected—and where are those connections missing?
- How are instructional materials reinforcing or challenging dominant narratives?
- In what ways are we leveraging bilingualism as a strength rather than treating it as a hurdle?
- How often do students' lived experiences shape classroom dialogue and learning tasks?

Then What?

In the short term, classrooms feel more responsive and inclusive. Hispanic students participate more readily, engage more deeply with content, and demonstrate increased confidence in sharing their thinking. Teachers observe stronger connections between academic concepts and students' real-world understanding, leading to more meaningful learning conversations.

Over time, culturally relevant instruction reshapes school culture. Teams begin to examine curriculum, assessments, and instructional routines through an equity lens, asking whose voices are centered and whose are missing. As this practice becomes embedded, schools see improved engagement, stronger academic identity, and instructional coherence that honors diversity without lowering expectations.

What If?

What if educators worry about making cultural missteps or feel unprepared to teach bilingually or across cultures? Discomfort is a natural part of growth. The goal is not perfection, but intentionality and reflection.

Schools can support this work through collaborative planning, professional learning, and peer modeling. Encouraging educators to learn alongside students, seek feedback, and refine practice builds confidence over time. When adults commit to learning with humility, culturally relevant instruction becomes a shared journey rather than an individual burden.

Way 22 — Family and Community Engagement: Partnership as Practice

What?

This Way reframes family and community engagement as a shared responsibility rather than a supplemental activity. For Hispanic students, families and community networks are often central to identity, decision-making, and resilience. Effective engagement recognizes families not as external stakeholders, but as essential partners in learning whose knowledge, language, and lived experience strengthen educational outcomes.

Family and community engagement is not limited to attendance at school events or compliance with school systems. It is an ongoing practice of relationship-building that centers trust, accessibility, and respect. **Resource 6.1: Cultural Celebration Toolkit** can help schools intentionally design engagement efforts that honor cultural values, linguistic diversity, and family realities, which in turn create conditions in which students experience coherence between home, school, and community.

Why?

Research consistently shows that strong family engagement is associated with improved attendance, academic performance, and social-emotional development. When families feel welcomed and included, they are more likely to advocate for their children, reinforce learning at home, and partner with schools to address challenges early. For Hispanic students, whose families may have experienced barriers related to language, immigration status, or prior schooling experiences, trust is especially critical.

When engagement efforts rely on one-way communication or assume families will adapt to school structures, participation often declines. Families may want to be involved but face obstacles such as work schedules, transportation, or language access. Intentional, culturally responsive engagement disrupts this pattern by shifting the burden of access from families to schools. When families feel respected and heard, students benefit from stronger support systems that extend beyond the classroom.

How?
Building meaningful family and community partnerships requires intentional design choices that remove barriers and center accessibility. These steps focus on what schools and educators can do to create inclusive engagement structures.

1. Design engagement opportunities with accessibility in mind
Plan events, meetings, and learning opportunities that account for language, schedules, and transportation realities. Offering bilingual formats, interpreters, and varied meeting times signals that families are expected and valued, not accommodated as an afterthought.

2. Communicate consistently and in culturally responsive ways
Use multiple communication methods—texts, emails, phone calls, and newsletters in families' preferred languages. See **Resource 6.2: Parent Newsletter Template** Clear, respectful communication builds trust and keeps families informed without requiring them to navigate unfamiliar systems.

3. Leverage community partnerships as extensions of learning
Partner with local organizations, cultural centers, faith-based

groups, or mentors to provide tutoring, enrichment, or family supports. Community partnerships expand learning opportunities while reinforcing that schools do not work in isolation.

4. Create spaces for family voice and leadership

Invite families to share perspectives, feedback, and ideas through advisory groups, surveys, or listening sessions. Engagement deepens when families see that their input shapes decisions rather than simply responding to them.

Reflection Prompts

- Which families have we intentionally connected with this week, and who might still feel on the margins?
- How accessible is our communication across language groups and formats?
- Where could community partnerships strengthen academic or social-emotional supports?
- In what ways are families positioned as contributors, not just recipients, of information?

Then What?

In the short term, schools see increased participation and more responsive communication between home and school. Families feel more confident reaching out with questions or concerns, and educators gain insight into students' strengths, needs, and contexts. Students benefit from consistent messaging and support across settings.

Over time, engagement becomes embedded in school culture rather than dependent on individual effort. Schools track participation patterns, adjust outreach strategies, and use feedback to refine programming. As trust grows, families and community partners become active collaborators in student success, reinforcing learning and well-being beyond the school day.

What If?

What if families are unable to attend events due to work schedules, childcare needs, or transportation barriers? Engagement does not have to be limited to in-person participation. Schools can offer virtual sessions, flexible meeting times, childcare options, or community-based meeting locations. By meeting families where they are, schools demonstrate respect for family realities and sustain partnerships that support student learning over time.

Way 23 — Supporting English Learners: Language Access Without Lowering Rigor

What?

This Way centers the responsibility of ensuring English Learners (ELs) have full access to rigorous instruction while developing academic language proficiency. Supporting English Learners is not about simplifying content or slowing expectations; it is about intentionally designing instruction so language is not a barrier to demonstrating thinking, reasoning, and understanding. ELs bring strong cognitive abilities, multilingual assets, and diverse perspectives that enrich learning when instruction is designed with access in mind.

Effective support for English Learners requires educators to separate language development from intellectual capacity. Too often, language proficiency is mistaken for a lack of understanding, leading to reduced academic challenge. This Way reframes support as strategic scaffolding—temporary structures that allow students to engage deeply with grade-level content while building confidence and independence as language skills grow.

Why?

Without intentional instructional scaffolds, English Learners may struggle to access content not because of a lack of ability, but because language demands obscure their thinking. Research by August and Shanahan (2023) emphasizes that structured language support significantly improves both academic achievement and engagement for English Learners. When instruction intentionally integrates language development with content learning, students are more likely to persist, participate, and succeed.

For English Learners, classrooms that prioritize speed, volume of language, or unstructured discussion can unintentionally limit access. Over time, this can result in gaps in achievement, confidence, and participation. Intentional support interrupts this pattern by ensuring students can demonstrate understanding through multiple modalities while developing academic English. When educators design with language access in mind, rigor is preserved and opportunity expands.

How?

Supporting English Learners requires deliberate instructional choices that make language visible and manageable without diluting expectations. These steps focus on adult design decisions that increase access and promote independence over time.

1. Make academic language explicit and visible

Use visual aids, sentence frames, word banks, and bilingual glossaries to clarify key concepts and vocabulary. Making language visible, **Resource 6.3: Bilingual Vocabulary Charts** supports comprehension while allowing students to engage with grade-level ideas from the start.

2. Structure collaborative learning intentionally

Pair English Learners with peers for discussion and problem-solving using clear roles or prompts. Structured collaboration provides language models and lowers the risk of participation while reinforcing content understanding.

3. Offer multiple modes for demonstrating understanding

Allow students to express thinking orally, in writing, or visually through drawings, diagrams, or digital tools. Multiple modes ensure language development does not limit students' ability to show what they know.

4. Gradually release scaffolds to build independence

Intentionally fade supports as students gain confidence and proficiency. Scaffolds should evolve over time, reinforcing growth rather than creating dependence. **Resource 6.4 EL Scaffolding Matrix** is a useful tool for planning and creating instructional groups.

Reflection Prompts

- Which English Learners need specific scaffolds this week, and which supports could be reduced to encourage independence?
- How are discussion structures ensuring every student can participate meaningfully?
- In what ways are we distinguishing between language development and conceptual understanding?
- How do instructional routines affirm bilingualism as an asset rather than a challenge?

Then What?

In the short term, English Learners participate more actively in lessons, discussions, and collaborative tasks. Teachers gain clearer insight into students' thinking, and students demonstrate increased confidence when engaging with complex content. Formative assessments begin to reflect understanding more accurately as language barriers are reduced. **Resource 6.5: Reflection Logs** organizes this student growth.

Over time, schools see stronger academic outcomes and more equitable participation for English Learners. Teams use data on both language proficiency and content mastery to refine instruction, adjust groupings, and calibrate supports. As scaffolding becomes intentional and responsive, English Learners experience consistent access to rigorous learning environments that value both language growth and intellectual challenge.

What If?

What if students resist using English in class or feel self-conscious about making mistakes? This response is common and reflects vulnerability rather than disengagement. Educators can normalize language development by celebrating bilingual responses, modeling risk-taking, and providing low-stakes opportunities for practice. When classrooms prioritize growth over perfection, students are more willing to participate, practice, and build confidence over time.

Way 24 — Celebrating Identity and Strengths: Affirmation as Instructional Practice

What?

This Way positions the celebration of identity and strengths as an intentional instructional practice rather than a symbolic gesture. For Hispanic students, cultural identity, language, family traditions, and community connections are not peripheral to learning—they are foundational assets that shape how students see themselves as learners. Celebrating identity means affirming students' lived experiences and talents in ways that reinforce belonging, confidence, and academic engagement.

This work goes beyond cultural holidays or surface-level recognition. It involves designing learning environments where students' languages, histories, and strengths are visible and valued every day. When educators intentionally recognize who students are and what they bring, they send a clear message: success does not require students to leave their identities at the door. Instead, identity becomes a source of pride and possibility within rigorous academic spaces.

Why?

Students are more motivated, engaged, and resilient when they feel seen and valued. Research on culturally responsive teaching underscores that identity affirmation strengthens academic identity and persistence by positioning culture and language as strengths rather than barriers (Gay, 2018). When students recognize that their identities are respected and celebrated, they are more willing to participate, take risks, and invest in learning.

For many Hispanic students, school experiences may have implicitly or explicitly minimized cultural expression or multilingualism. Over time, this can erode confidence and reinforce the false idea that academic success requires assimilation. Intentional celebration of identity disrupts this narrative. It reinforces that high expectations and cultural affirmation coexist—and that students' talents, leadership, and community contributions are integral to learning, not distractions from it.

How?

Celebrating identity and strengths requires thoughtful instructional and cultural design choices. These steps focus on adult

actions that embed affirmation into daily practice rather than isolating it to special events.

1.   Embed cultural relevance into core learning tasks
Design projects, discussions, and assessments that allow students
to draw on cultural knowledge, histories, and experiences as part of
academic work. This might include culturally relevant case studies,
historical perspectives, or artistic expression connected to learning
goals.

**2.   Normalize and celebrate multilingualism as an academic
strength**
 Publicly affirm bilingual and multilingual abilities through classroom routines, displays, and language use. Highlighting language
as an asset reinforces that students' full linguistic repertoires are
valued in academic spaces.

3.   Recognize strengths beyond traditional academic measures
Intentionally acknowledge leadership, collaboration, creativity, perseverance, and community involvement. Broadening what counts
as "success" affirms diverse talents and reinforces that learning is
multidimensional.

4.   Create student-centered opportunities for sharing identity
Offer structured opportunities for students to share stories, projects, or experiences in ways that feel authentic and voluntary.
When students control how they share their identities, affirmation
becomes empowering rather than performative.

Reflection Prompts
- Where do Hispanic students see their identities and
  strengths reflected in our daily instructional practices?
- How are we recognizing talents and contributions beyond
  grades and test scores?

+ In what ways are students invited to shape how their culture and language are represented in class?
+ How do our recognition practices reinforce dignity rather than tokenism?

Then What?

In the short term, classrooms become more inclusive and affirming. Hispanic students participate more confidently, take academic risks, and demonstrate greater ownership of their learning. Teachers notice stronger relationships and more authentic engagement as students see their identities reflected in meaningful ways.

Over time, celebrating identity and strengths contributes to a school culture rooted in belonging and high expectations. Schools collect student feedback to refine recognition practices and expand opportunities for student-led showcases, exhibitions, or cultural events. As affirmation becomes embedded in instruction, students develop stronger academic identities and a clearer sense that who they are is inseparable from how they learn.

What If?

What if students feel uncomfortable with public recognition or worry about being singled out? Affirmation should never feel forced. Educators can offer multiple options for recognition, including private acknowledgments or small-group celebrations, and allow students to choose how they share their achievements. When students have agency in how their identities and strengths are recognized, celebration becomes a source of confidence rather than discomfort.

Closing Reflection

Miguel's journey mirrors the experiences of many Hispanic students navigating school, home, and community responsibilities. As leaders and educators, we are called to see students holistically—acknowledging their strengths, supporting their challenges, and creating inclusive opportunities for learning.

By embedding culturally relevant instruction, scaffolding language supports, and engaging families meaningfully, schools send a powerful message: Hispanic students belong, their voices matter, and their success is a shared priority. Closing the achievement gap requires consistent action, reflection, and collaboration.

The Constellation of Learning™ Synopsis

Aligned with **Instructional Coherence & High-Quality Teaching**, this chapter emphasizes how Hispanic students flourish when instruction and identity are woven together. Coherence here means embracing linguistic and cultural assets as academic capital rather than challenges to overcome. Language is not a limitation—it's a legacy to honor.

When schools connect home culture to classroom rigor, engagement deepens. Bilingualism, family involvement, and heritage-infused instruction are not additions to coherence—they are its essence. By centering instruction around identity, educators create learning that sustains both achievement and pride.

Hallway Confessions – Daily Practice and Perspective

Some teachers walk into the classroom worried they'll say the wrong thing, mispronounce a student's name, or stumble through a bilingual instruction moment. We get it—that pressure is real. But the truth? Kids notice effort, not perfection. We once watched a teacher carefully try to pronounce every Spanish name in her roster. She stumbled, apologized, and tried again the next day. By the third week, students were laughing with her, not at her, and participation soared. Effort builds trust.

Another teacher confided that she felt guilty for not having enough bilingual resources. She was teaching science with mostly English texts. So she started small: a vocabulary board with key terms in English and Spanish, short bilingual mini-lessons, and peer discussion in both languages. Students thrived, and she discovered the joy in seeing students connect concepts across languages.

Finally, we've seen teachers overthink engagement, trying to create elaborate activities every day. But often, a simple check-in, a warm smile, or asking a student to explain their thinking in Spanish first, then English, makes a bigger difference. Authenticity beats perfection every time. When we show curiosity, listen respectfully, and honor identity, trust builds learning."

This reflection reminds educators that equity is not an add-on—it is embedded in the daily decisions, classroom structures, and leadership practices that shape the educational environment.

The Dismissal Bell – The Five A's

When the final bell rings, we must ask whether students leave school having used their language—or left it at the door. For many Hispanic students, identity, family, and learning are inseparable from language. When schools treat bilingualism as a barrier to manage rather than an asset to build, students learn to shrink parts of themselves in order to succeed. But when educators honor home language, partner authentically with families, and design instruction that affirms cultural identity, students leave stronger, more confident, and more connected. Equity takes root when students no longer have to choose between who they are and how they learn—and when families are welcomed as essential partners in that journey.

Action Step	Description
Audit	Examine current practices and student outcomes for Hispanic students. Review attendance, graduation rates, English Learner growth, and participation in enrichment programs.
Adjust	Identify gaps in instruction, language scaffolds, family engagement, and cultural representation. Implement targeted interventions where needed.
Advocate	Promote policies and programs that support bilingual education, culturally responsive pedagogy, and equitable access to resources. Be a voice for Hispanic students at all levels of decision-making.
Assemble	Collaboratively engage staff, families, and community partners to implement sustainable practices. Establish teams, share responsibilities, and coordinate efforts to support students collectively.
Attitude Ask	Approach every decision with empathy, humility, and persistence. Believe in students' potential and maintain a mindset that celebrates culture, language, and identity as assets, not obstacles.

Native American Students: Restoring Voice, Reviving Tradition, and Reclaiming Space

This chapter invites educators to slow down, listen more deeply, and reconsider what it means to teach responsibly within histories that long predate our schools. Education, in this context, is inseparable from land, memory, and story. Honoring the land in our teaching is how we honor the ancestors whose stories still shape our classrooms.

> Honoring the land in our teaching is how we honor the ancestors whose stories still shape our classrooms.

Opening Vignette

It's early October, and the morning sun illuminates the hallways of Pine Ridge Community School. Jace, a fifteen-year-old student of Lakota heritage, walks quietly to his locker. His backpack is heavy with books, but heavier still are the expectations he carries. His father works two jobs to support the family, while his grandmother, a storyteller and keeper of family history, insists he honor their traditions even as he navigates school expectations.

Above his locker, a poster reads: *"Your voice matters. Your story matters."* He smiles faintly. For some students in his community, these words are more than encouragement—they are a reminder that education has often overlooked students like him. His science teacher, Mrs. Tallbear, pauses at the doorway, greeting him warmly in Lakota before English. For a moment, Jace feels seen.

Later in class, the lesson turns to environmental science. Jace's group discusses the local river and its significance to their ancestors. He explains how pollution has affected the land his people have cared for across generations, and the teacher encourages the class to reflect on cultural knowledge alongside scientific methods. That day, Jace doesn't just learn chemistry—he shares a part of himself, bridging two worlds.

This vignette illustrates the realities Native American students face: balancing cultural heritage, academic expectations, and community challenges. Their experiences highlight the need for culturally responsive practices that honor identity while fostering academic success.

Framing the Challenge

Native American students are among the most underserved in the U.S. education system, yet they demonstrate resilience and cultural wealth. According to the National Center for Education Statistics (2023), approximately 1.1 million students identify as Native American, just over 1.5% of the total student population (NCES, 2023). Despite their small proportion, they experience disproportionate challenges, including high rates of chronic absenteeism, limited access to advanced coursework, and lower graduation rates. In 2022, the four-year high school graduation rate for Native American students was 75%, compared with 88% for all students (U.S. Department of Education, 2023).

Geography compounds these challenges. Many students attend schools on reservations or in rural areas with limited access to educational resources, technology, and extracurricular opportunities. The National Indian Education Study (2022) reports over 60% of students in tribal schools feel the curriculum does not sufficiently incorporate Native history, language, or culture, contributing to disengagement. Research shows that integrating cultural knowledge improves engagement, academic achievement, and self-esteem (Pierce, 2022; Lomawaima & McCarty, 2023).

Social-emotional factors are equally critical. Native youth report higher rates of trauma exposure, including historical and intergenerational trauma, correlating with stress, absenteeism, and mental health challenges (Brave Heart, 2022). Despite these obstacles, students demonstrate strong community engagement, resilience, and leadership capacities when schools validate their identities and provide culturally sustaining support.

This context underscores the need for targeted strategies addressing inequities, honoring cultural knowledge, and providing holistic support. Effective practices include integrating tribal histories, fostering family and community partnerships, and implementing mentorship systems that elevate students' unique strengths. The four actionable "Ways" in this chapter are grounded in research and designed to create environments where Native American students can thrive academically, socially, and culturally.

Way 25 — Honoring Tribal Knowledge and Histories: Centering Indigenous Voices in Learning

What?

This Way calls educators to intentionally honor tribal knowledge and histories by centering Native American perspectives, languages, stories, and practices within curriculum and instruction. For Native students, learning is most meaningful when their heritage is not treated as an add-on or historical footnote, but as living knowledge that continues to shape identity, community, and ways of knowing. Honoring tribal knowledge means recognizing Indigenous knowledge systems as valid, rigorous, and essential to a complete understanding of the world.

This work goes beyond symbolic recognition or isolated cultural lessons. It requires educators to examine whose voices are represented in curriculum, whose stories are told, and whose knowledge is considered authoritative. When Native students see their cultures and histories reflected accurately and respectfully, school becomes a place of affirmation rather than erasure.

Why?

Research on culturally sustaining pedagogy emphasizes that authentic representation improves student engagement, strengthens self-esteem, and supports academic outcomes. Lomawaima and McCarty (2023) highlight that when Indigenous students experience instruction grounded in their cultural contexts, they are more likely to feel a sense of belonging and connection to school. Authentic inclusion of Native histories and perspectives also helps counteract centuries of misrepresentation and invisibility within formal education systems.

Data from the *National Indian Education Study* (2022) further reinforces this need, finding that Native students exposed to culturally relevant curriculum reported a twenty-five percent increase in engagement compared to peers who experienced more traditional instruction. These findings underscore that honoring tribal knowledge is not solely about cultural affirmation—it is an academic imperative. Beginning with self-examination, **Resource 7.1: Equity & Belonging Reflection Tool** supports educators in examining beliefs and practices that shape inclusion while giving necessary look-fors to guide instructional and cultural decisions.

Resource 7.1: Equity & Belonging Reflection Checklist

Focus Area	Reflection Questions
Curriculum Representation	◆ Do instructional materials reflect Native American peoples as contemporary communities, not only historical groups? ◆ Are Native voices, authors, or perspectives included in ways that honor accuracy and sovereignty?
Classroom Environment	◆ Do classroom visuals and displays avoid stereotypes and instead affirm authentic Native identities? ◆ Are land acknowledgments, symbols, or references used thoughtfully rather than decoratively?
Instructional Practices	◆ Do learning experiences honor multiple ways of knowing, including storytelling, observation, and relational learning? ◆ Are students able to demonstrate understanding through varied formats beyond traditional written responses?
Student Voice	◆ Do Native American students have opportunities to lead, contribute, or share perspectives by choice—not expectation? ◆ Are student contributions affirmed without positioning students as representatives for an entire culture?
Family & Community Connection	◆ Are tribal families and communities viewed as partners with expertise, not just participants? ◆ Are communication and engagement practices respectful of tribal sovereignty, traditions, and boundaries?

How?

Honoring tribal knowledge requires intentional planning, humility, and collaboration. These steps focus on adult design decisions that respect sovereignty, accuracy, and lived cultural experience.

1. **Partner with tribal elders and cultural liaisons**
Collaborate with local tribal leaders, elders, or cultural liaisons to ensure instruction reflects accurate histories and respectful practices. These partnerships help educators avoid assumptions and honor community voice as central to curriculum design.

2. **Integrate Native languages into learning environments**
Incorporate Native languages into classroom signage, greetings, projects, or learning routines when appropriate. Language visibility affirms identity and communicates respect for Indigenous knowledge systems.

3. **Center storytelling and oral histories as legitimate texts**
Dedicate instructional time to storytelling and oral histories as sources of knowledge, not supplements. Oral traditions carry cultural, historical, and moral understanding that deepen learning across disciplines.

4. **Use Native-authored resources and media**
Select textbooks, literature, and digital media created by Native authors and scholars. Native-authored materials ensure accuracy, complexity, and representation grounded in lived experience rather than external interpretation.

Reflection Prompts

- How does our current curriculum reflect—or ignore—Native histories, perspectives, and contributions?
- Where might misrepresentation or omission be shaping student understanding?

- What opportunities exist for Native students to share cultural knowledge in ways that feel respectful and voluntary?
- How are adult assumptions influencing what is taught and what is left out?

Then What?

In the short term, classrooms become spaces where Native students feel seen and respected. Students engage more fully when their cultures and histories are treated as integral to learning rather than peripheral. Teachers gain deeper insight into students' identities and the cultural contexts that shape learning.

Over time, honoring tribal knowledge contributes to stronger school–community relationships and more inclusive curriculum practices. Schools begin by integrating tribal knowledge into a single unit or lesson, then expand intentionally. As partnerships deepen and instructional practices evolve, schools foster learning environments that affirm Native identity, support engagement, and strengthen academic belonging.

What If?

What if educators worry about accuracy or fear causing harm through misrepresentation? Caution is appropriate and necessary. Schools can address this by partnering with tribal education departments, cultural liaisons, or Native scholars who can guide curriculum decisions. When resources feel limited, educators can use reputable digital archives and Native-authored content to supplement instruction. If resistance arises, grounding conversations in research on engagement and outcomes helps reframe this work as essential rather than optional.

Way 26 — Building Bridges with Families and Tribal Communities: Partnership Rooted in Relationship

What?

This Way positions family and tribal community engagement as a shared, reciprocal partnership grounded in respect, trust, and cultural understanding. For Native American students, families and tribal communities are not external supports—they are central to identity, learning, and well-being. Building bridges means moving beyond transactional communication to sustained relationships that honor sovereignty, cultural protocols, and community wisdom.

Authentic engagement requires schools to see themselves not as isolated institutions, but as part of a broader ecosystem that invests in youth, programs, and collective vision. When educators intentionally partner with families and tribal communities, learning becomes more coherent and culturally grounded. This Way emphasizes engagement that is ongoing, relational, and rooted in mutual accountability rather than one-time events or compliance-driven outreach.

Why?

Research consistently shows that engagement with families and tribal leaders is associated with higher attendance, improved academic performance, and stronger student identity. Brayboy and Maughan (2023) emphasize that culturally grounded partnerships enhance students' sense of belonging and reinforce learning by aligning school practices with community values and expectations. These relationships also provide critical insight that helps educators design instruction and support systems that are responsive rather than assumptive.

For Native students, historical mistrust of educational systems can create barriers to engagement. When schools fail to acknowledge past harms or ignore cultural protocols, families may disengage as a protective response. Intentional partnership-building disrupts this cycle by demonstrating respect, transparency, and shared purpose. Engagement rooted in relationship, rather than obligation, strengthens student outcomes and community trust simultaneously.

How?

Building bridges with families and tribal communities requires deliberate actions that prioritize listening, accessibility, and shared leadership. These steps focus on adult decisions that create conditions for authentic collaboration.

1. Establish consistent, culturally respectful communication

Communicate regularly through newsletters, meetings, and digital platforms in ways that honor preferred languages, protocols, and communication norms. Consistency signals commitment and reduces barriers to engagement.

2. Invite families and tribal leaders into shared decision-making

Include families and tribal representatives on advisory councils, curriculum review teams, or planning committees. Shared leadership ensures that decisions reflect community priorities and cultural context.

3. Create opportunities for community-centered gatherings

Host cultural events, celebrations, or learning showcases that center Native traditions and knowledge. These gatherings should prioritize relationship-building and shared learning over performance or publicity.

4. Learn from families through home and community visits
When appropriate and respectful, conduct home or community visits to better understand students' contexts and strengths. Listening in these spaces deepens empathy and informs more responsive school practices.

5. Connect students with culturally responsive mentorship
Partner with community members to create mentorship opportunities that affirm identity and leadership. Grounded in relationship-building, **Resource 7.2: Mentorship Program Templates** promote culturally responsive connections that extend learning beyond the classroom.

Reflection Prompts
+ How are families and tribal communities currently involved in meaningful decision-making?
+ What barriers—structural, cultural, or historical—may be limiting engagement?
+ In what ways do our engagement practices reflect respect for sovereignty and protocol?
+ How are community voices shaping instructional and support strategies?

Then What?
In the short term, schools see increased trust and participation from families and tribal partners. Communication becomes more two-way, and educators gain deeper insight into student strengths, needs, and cultural contexts. Students benefit from consistent messaging and support across school and community settings.

Over time, engagement evolves into sustained partnership. Schools identify key community members to support a focused initiative, evaluate outcomes, and expand collaboration intentionally. As relationships deepen, schools function as hubs within a larger community network invested in youth development, academic success, and cultural affirmation.

What If?

What if families are hesitant to engage due to past experiences or mistrust? Trust must be earned through patience, consistency, and respect. Schools can build trust by meeting families where they are, offering flexible engagement options, and honoring cultural protocols. When staff feel unfamiliar with community expectations, targeted professional learning can build confidence and competence. Logistical challenges can be addressed through virtual or hybrid methods that expand access while maintaining connection.

Way 27 — Implementing Culturally Responsive Curriculum: Designing Learning That Honors Ways of Knowing

What?

This Way defines culturally responsive curriculum as an intentional design practice that honors students' cultural contexts, histories, and ways of knowing as essential to academic learning. For Native American students, a culturally responsive curriculum integrates Indigenous epistemologies, ethical frameworks, environmental stewardship, and tribal histories alongside academic content. Learning is connected to place, community, and lived experience rather than isolated from them.

Culturally responsive curriculum moves beyond surface-level inclusion. It asks educators to examine whose knowledge is centered, whose perspectives are validated, and how instruction positions Native students as intellectual contributors rather than passive recipients of information. When curriculum reflects

Indigenous knowledge systems with accuracy and respect, students experience learning as relevant, rigorous, and affirming.

Why?

Research and practice show that culturally responsive curriculum increases engagement, comprehension, and retention while reducing opportunity gaps. Students who see themselves reflected in curriculum are more likely to participate actively, persist through challenge, and develop stronger academic identities. For Native American students, representation is closely tied to belonging, motivation, and trust in schooling systems.

When Indigenous perspectives are omitted or misrepresented, students may disengage or internalize the message that their knowledge and histories are secondary. Implementing culturally responsive curriculum disrupts this pattern by validating Native ways of knowing as rigorous and meaningful. When instruction affirms identity and intellect together, learning becomes more durable and impactful.

How?

Implementing culturally responsive curriculum requires intentional planning and sustained reflection. The following steps focus on adult design decisions that embed cultural relevance into core instruction.

1. Audit curriculum for representation and opportunity

Examine existing units, texts, and materials to identify where Native perspectives are present, absent, or inaccurately portrayed. Curriculum audits help teams identify opportunities for meaningful integration rather than symbolic inclusion.

2. Design project-based learning connected to community challenges

Develop learning experiences that address real-world issues relevant to Native communities, such as environmental stewardship, land use, or community well-being. Project-based learning allows students to apply academic skills while drawing on cultural knowledge and values.

3. Integrate Indigenous perspectives across disciplines

Ensure Native knowledge systems appear across subject areas—not only in social studies. Science, mathematics, language arts, and the arts all offer opportunities to include Indigenous problem-solving, ethical reasoning, and worldviews.

4. Provide student choice grounded in cultural connection

Offer students options to connect learning to their cultural experiences, interests, or community knowledge. Choice reinforces agency and affirms that cultural background is an academic asset.

5. Align assessments to honor rigor and cultural understanding

Design assessments that allow students to demonstrate mastery through multiple modalities while honoring cultural context. Alignment ensures academic rigor is maintained while access and relevance are expanded. By centering Native-authored voices, **Resource 7.3: Native-Authored Curriculum & Media List** ensures curriculum representation is authentic, accurate, and grounded in lived experience rather than external interpretation.

Reflection Prompts

- How does our current curriculum reflect—or overlook—Native perspectives and ways of knowing?
- Which lessons or units could be redesigned to better connect learning to community and place?
- Where might curriculum unintentionally reinforce dominant narratives at the expense of Indigenous knowledge?

+ How are students given agency to connect academic content to cultural understanding?

Then What?

In the short term, piloting one culturally responsive unit increases student engagement and participation. Educators collect feedback from students and, when appropriate, community partners to refine instruction and materials. Learning conversations become richer as students draw connections between content and lived experience.

Over time, culturally responsive curriculum becomes embedded across grade levels and disciplines. Schools expand implementation gradually, ensuring alignment with standards while honoring cultural integrity. As this work deepens, Native students experience stronger academic identity, increased engagement, and more consistent access to rigorous, relevant learning.

What If?

What if staff express resistance or uncertainty about redesigning curriculum? Resistance often reflects unfamiliarity rather than opposition. Schools can respond with professional learning grounded in research and concrete examples of culturally responsive practice. When resources feel limited, open-source materials and Native-authored digital content provide accessible entry points. Testing pressures can be addressed by intentionally aligning culturally responsive curriculum to standards, reinforcing that rigor and relevance are mutually reinforcing.

Way 28 — Providing Mentorship and Identity Support: Relationships That Sustain Belonging

What?

This Way centers mentorship and identity support as essential structures for student success rather than supplemental programs. For Native American students, mentorship builds sustained relationships with adults who understand, respect, and affirm cultural identity while supporting academic growth. Identity support ensures that students are not asked to separate who they are from who they are becoming as learners and leaders.

Mentorship is most powerful when it is culturally grounded and relational rather than transactional. When students have access to adults who recognize their cultural contexts, honor tribal values, and model pathways for success, school becomes a place of possibility rather than isolation. This Way positions mentorship as a protective and empowering force that strengthens belonging, confidence, and persistence.

Why?

Research consistently demonstrates that mentorship improves attendance, engagement, and social-emotional outcomes. Students who participate in mentorship programs show higher levels of persistence, confidence, and academic motivation. For Native American students, mentorship also supports identity development by reinforcing cultural pride and countering narratives of invisibility or marginalization.

Without intentional mentorship structures, students may navigate school without consistent adult advocacy or guidance. Over time, this can contribute to disengagement or diminished self-belief. Identity-affirming mentorship interrupts this trajectory by providing trusted relationships that help students navigate challenges, envision futures, and remain connected to school. When mentorship is embedded into school design, it becomes a stabilizing force that supports long-term success.

How?

Providing meaningful mentorship and identity support requires intentional structures and consistent adult commitment. These steps focus on adult actions that create sustained, culturally responsive relationships.

1. Pair students with culturally informed mentors

Match students with mentors who understand Native cultural contexts or are committed to learning from them. Mentors may include educators, community members, elders, or alumni who can offer guidance grounded in respect and lived experience.

2. Establish regular, predictable check-ins

Schedule consistent meeting times to build trust and continuity. Predictability strengthens relationships and signals to students that mentorship is a priority rather than an occasional interaction.

3. Facilitate identity-affirming spaces and conversations

Create opportunities such as circles or small-group discussions where students can explore identity, belonging, and leadership in safe, respectful environments. These spaces affirm heritage while supporting personal and academic growth.

4. Provide academic and career guidance rooted in relevance

Support students in exploring academic pathways, careers, and goals that connect to their interests and community values. Guidance becomes more meaningful when it aligns with students' identities and aspirations.

5. Encourage peer mentorship and leadership

Build structures that allow students to mentor and support one another. Peer mentorship reinforces leadership, strengthens community, and extends support beyond adult-student relationships.

Reflection Prompts

- Are mentorship opportunities accessible to all Native students, or only a few?
- How intentionally is identity support embedded within mentorship structures?
- Whose voices and experiences are represented among mentors?
- How do mentorship relationships reinforce belonging and agency?

Then What?

In the short term, schools launch a pilot mentorship program and gather feedback from students, mentors, and families. Students report stronger relationships with adults, increased confidence, and greater engagement with school. Educators gain insight into students' strengths, needs, and aspirations beyond academic data.

Over time, mentorship expands through community partnership. **Resource 7.4: Community Engagement Guide** strengthens collaboration with families, tribal organizations, and community partners to broaden mentoring networks. Sustained through shared leadership, **Resource 7.5: Advisory Council Framework** centers elder, advisor, and community voice in school decision-making, ensuring mentorship remains culturally grounded and responsive.

What If?

What if there are limited mentors available? Schools can expand access through virtual mentoring, alumni networks, or partnerships with tribal and community organizations. If students are hesitant to participate, beginning with informal activities helps build trust before formal mentoring structures are introduced. When administrative support is uncertain, grounding conversations in evidence linking mentorship to attendance, engagement, and long-term outcomes helps reinforce this work as essential rather than optional.

Closing Reflection

Jace's project integrates tribal environmental knowledge, mentorship builds confidence, and curriculum reflects heritage. Schools honoring tribal knowledge, engaging families, implementing responsive curricula, and providing mentorship foster resilience, engagement, and achievement. Intentionality, empathy, and collaboration are essential for Native student success.

The Constellation of Learning™ Synopsis

This chapter reflects the power of **Whole-School & Community Well-Being**, urging us to restore relationships with Native communities through respect, reciprocity, and relevance. Well-being in this constellation is collective—it thrives when schools honor indigenous histories, amplify voices, and co-create with families rather than speak for them.

To sustain well-being, educators must understand that culture is not content; it's context. When instruction honors place, story, and tradition, it heals the disconnection many Native students experience. Education becomes ceremony—a shared commitment to continuity, respect, and renewal.

Hallway Confessions – Daily Practice & Perspective

Teaching Native American students requires mindfulness in every classroom interaction. In one hallway conversation, a teacher reflected with Adam. "I worry about mispronouncing student names or not fully understanding their cultural context. But I've learned that students notice effort more than perfection. It's about showing curiosity, listening respectfully, and valuing their experiences."

Another educator shared with us: "I realized small gestures make a difference. Greeting students in their tribal language, including references to their community in lessons, or celebrating culturally significant events strengthens trust. Students respond positively when they feel their identity is seen."

Daily practices include checking in with students about their experiences, connecting academic content to local cultural knowledge, and intentionally designing lessons to include Indigenous perspectives. Teachers note that consistent routines that honor tribal practices—like starting a morning circle with stories or reflections—help students feel a sense of belonging from the moment they enter the classroom.

Staff also discuss challenges: balancing curriculum requirements with cultural relevance, finding time for mentorship conversations, and integrating family perspectives into classroom activities. One teacher said, "Adjusting my lessons isn't just about content; it's about building relationships. Sometimes that means pausing the lesson to address a student's concern or asking how a project connects to their community."

Across hallways and classrooms, these small, intentional daily practices accumulate into a culture of respect, belonging, and engagement. Teachers report that when these routines are consistent, students are more engaged, confident, and willing to participate academically and socially.

The Dismissal Bell – The Five A's

When the final bell rings, we must ask whether Native American students leave school having been honored—or erased. Too often, they move through classrooms where their histories are minimized, their sovereignty misunderstood, and their identities treated as peripheral rather than foundational. These experiences are not incidental; they reflect systems that were never designed with Native students in mind. When educators restore voice, honor cultural knowledge, and build authentic partnerships with Native communities, schools become spaces of respect rather than replacement. Equity is realized when Native students see their stories, languages, and traditions reflected with accuracy and dignity—and when belonging is reclaimed, not granted.

Action Step	Description
Audit	Examine curriculum, mentorship access, family engagement, and outcomes.
Adjust	Implement culturally sustaining lessons and mentorship programs.
Advocate	Engage tribal councils, families, and community partners.
Assemble	Build mentorship circles, advisory boards, cultural events, and PLCs.
Attitude Ask	Commit to culturally responsive practices ensuring students are fully seen and supported.

CHAPTER 8

LGBTQIA+ Students: Belonging Without Exception

Opening Vignette

When Lucas came out at the end of the semester, his English Language Arts teacher didn't know what to expect. He'd always been a thoughtful presence in class—quiet, observant, but quick to smile. In the weeks leading up to our conversation, though, something changed. His eyes darted toward the door more often, his laughter faded, and his essays circled around identity.

One afternoon, he lingered after the bell rang, hands trembling slightly as he spoke. "I've been feeling this way for a while," he said. "I'm gay, and I don't know what to do with it." His voice cracked, equal parts fear and relief.

His teacher didn't fill the silence with advice. She listened, offering space and safety. "You don't have to figure it out alone," she told him. "You're safe here. You matter here."

The weight lifted almost visibly. Over the following weeks, Lucas began contributing more, volunteering for group projects, and smiling again. His courage quietly rippled across the classroom. Another student confided about being nonbinary. A third asked to include LGBTQIA+ authors in a literature circle. Lucas's voice became a spark that helped others see they weren't alone.

For students like Lucas, the issue isn't just coming out—it's being accepted once they do. When schools model inclusive, affirming environments, we don't just protect students; we help them thrive. Visibility, validation, and belonging are not luxuries. They're lifelines.

For many students, the greatest risk is not being seen too much, but not being seen at all. When identity is ignored or erased, belonging becomes conditional and learning suffers. Visibility is the first step toward validation—students can't flourish in shadows.

Framing the Challenge

Too often, LGBTQIA+ students navigate school systems that were never intentionally designed with their safety, identity, or belonging in mind. While many schools speak the language of inclusion, the daily experiences of LGBTQIA+ students tell a more complicated story. For too many of these students, hallways feel unsafe, classrooms feel silent when slurs are spoken, and policies feel neutral on paper but harmful in practice. Visibility does not automatically equal affirmation. And affirmation is not a luxury—it is foundational to learning. When students must scan the room before speaking, edit themselves before participating, or

> When students must scan the room before speaking, edit themselves before participating, or question whether adults will protect them, cognitive energy shifts from growth to survival.

question whether adults will protect them, cognitive energy shifts from growth to survival.

Across the nation, LGBTQIA+ students face disproportionate barriers to learning and well-being. According to *The Trevor Project's 2023 National Survey on LGBTQ Youth Mental Health*, forty-one percent of LGBTQIA+ youth seriously considered suicide in the past year, and nearly one in five attempted it. Rates were even higher among transgender and nonbinary youth (The Trevor Project, 2023).

Recent national surveys indicate that hostile school climates for LGBTQIA+ students remain widespread. In a 2023 Human Rights Campaign survey, nearly fifty-nine percent of LGBTQ+ youth reported being bullied, teased, or treated badly at school, and forty-six percent indicated they felt unsafe in at least one school setting (Human Rights Campaign, 2023). Similarly, the Trevor Project's 2023 U.S. National Survey found that a majority of LGBTQ+ youth experienced verbal harassment at school due to their sexual orientation or gender identity, with sixty percent reporting discrimination in the past year (The Trevor Project, 2023). While these conditions present significant risks to student well-being and learning, research consistently demonstrates that affirming school environments reduce harm and support stronger academic, social, and emotional outcomes.

Many students navigate school invisibly—present but unacknowledged. Some remain closeted for safety; others reveal only fragments of themselves. This invisibility erodes confidence, motivation, and belonging. Schools can counter it by building cultures that celebrate every identity rather than simply tolerating difference.

When LGBTQIA+ students feel seen and validated, engagement and achievement rise. Kosciw et al. (2022) found that inclusive curricula correlate with higher GPAs and stronger feelings of belonging. Inclusion is not political—it's pedagogical.

Neutrality is not neutrality; it's neglect. Ensuring every learner thrives means designing systems that affirm identity, confront bias, and cultivate dignity for all.

Way 29 — Cultivating an Inclusive, Affirming Environment: Safety as a Daily Practice

What?

This Way defines an inclusive, affirming environment as one where every student feels seen, safe, and valued—not occasionally, but consistently. For LGBTQIA+ students, inclusion extends far beyond symbolic gestures such as a pride flag or a single awareness week. Affirmation lives in daily language, curriculum choices, policies, and the tone adults set in classrooms and hallways.

Creating an affirming environment requires schools to examine both visible and invisible messages about belonging. This includes dismantling stereotypes, ensuring authentic LGBTQIA+ representation across learning experiences, and re-examining traditions or procedures—such as gendered dress codes or binary restroom policies—that may unintentionally signal exclusion. A truly affirming school culture communicates, often quietly but powerfully, *"You are welcome here, exactly as you are."*

Why?

Students whose identities are respected and affirmed experience stronger academic outcomes and improved well-being. According to GLSEN (2022), LGBTQIA+ students in affirming schools are fifty percent less likely to miss school due to safety concerns and twenty percent more likely to plan for postsecondary education. These findings highlight that inclusion is not an abstract value—it is a protective factor that directly influences access to learning.

Inclusive environments also benefit all students. Exposure to diverse identities and perspectives fosters empathy, critical thinking, and civic awareness—skills essential for academic success and democratic participation. When schools commit to affirmation, they create learning spaces where difference is not tolerated but respected, and where students are more willing to engage, collaborate, and grow.

How?

Cultivating an inclusive, affirming environment requires intentional adult action and sustained commitment. These steps focus on design choices educators and leaders control, not on asking students to self-advocate for basic safety.

1. Build staff capacity through intentional learning

Provide ongoing professional learning that goes beyond awareness to deepen understanding of LGBTQIA+ identities, intersectionality, and allyship. Sustained learning helps staff respond with confidence and care rather than hesitation or silence.

2. Integrate LGBTQIA+ representation across curriculum

Include LGBTQIA+ voices and perspectives throughout subject areas—literature, science, history, the arts—rather than isolating representation to specific units or months. Integration signals that LGBTQIA+ identities are part of the human story, not an exception.

3. Review policies and procedures through an inclusion lens

Audit handbooks, dress codes, restroom access, and participation policies for inclusivity. Providing gender-neutral options and clear pronoun protocols reduces ambiguity and increases safety for students navigating school systems.

4. Normalize inclusive language and practices
Model inclusive language such as "students" instead of gendered groupings. Invite pronoun sharing in ways that are voluntary and safe, recognizing that affirmation should never force disclosure.

5. Make belonging visible in learning spaces
Display inclusive visuals, texts, and classroom agreements that affirm identity and safety. In daily classroom practice **Resource 8.1: Inclusive Classroom Checklist** supports visible signals of safety, affirmation, and belonging that students experience consistently.

Reflection Prompts

- How do daily routines and language signal safety and belonging for LGBTQIA+ students?
- What hidden barriers might exist in classroom norms, policies, or traditions?
- Where are LGBTQIA+ identities visible—and where are they absent—in curriculum and materials?
- How are adults modeling inclusion when discomfort or uncertainty arises?

Then What?
In the short term, classrooms become calmer, safer spaces where LGBTQIA+ students participate more fully and experience reduced anxiety. Teachers notice stronger engagement, fewer behavioral disruptions rooted in stress, and improved peer interactions. Early indicators appear in attendance, classroom climate, and student feedback.

Over time, affirmation becomes embedded in school culture rather than dependent on individual champions. Schools use climate surveys, student voice forums, and ongoing reflection to assess impact and refine practices. Inclusion becomes iterative—continuously examined, strengthened, and sustained—so that safety and belonging remain non-negotiable conditions for learning.

What If?

What if resistance emerges from staff, families, or community members? Resistance often reflects fear or misunderstanding rather than malice.

Leaders can respond by grounding conversations in empathy and evidence, framing inclusion as student safety and well-being rather than ideology. Small, courageous actions—modeled consistently—shift culture over time. When adults lead with clarity and care, schools move closer to becoming places where every student can learn without fear.

Way 30 — Supporting LGBTQIA+ Students' Social-Emotional Well-Being: Care as a Condition for Learning

What?

This Way centers social-emotional well-being as a foundational condition for learning rather than a supplemental support. LGBTQIA+ students often navigate isolation, anxiety, or rejection inside and outside of school. According to *The Trevor Project* (2023), nearly sixty percent of LGBTQIA+ youth who wanted mental-health care were unable to access it. Schools cannot solve every external barrier, but they can create environments in which students experience care, connection, and emotional safety each day.

Social-emotional learning (SEL) for LGBTQIA+ students is not a separate initiative or program. It is a mindset expressed through relationships, routines, language, and adult responsiveness.

When SEL is embedded into daily practice, students experience school as a place where their emotions are acknowledged, their identities are affirmed, and their well-being matters as much as academic performance.

Why?

Emotional safety precedes academic success. Students who feel psychologically safe are more likely to attend school regularly, engage in learning, and persist through challenges. Research from CASEL (2022) confirms that strong SEL competencies are associated with improved mental health, stronger relationships, and increased academic achievement.

For LGBTQIA+ students, the absence of emotional support can quietly undermine learning. Fear of rejection or invisibility can consume cognitive and emotional energy, making academic engagement difficult. Intentional SEL practices buffer these stressors by reinforcing belonging and trust. When students believe adults care about their well-being, they are more willing to participate, ask for help, and invest in their learning.

How?

Supporting LGBTQIA+ students' social-emotional well-being requires intentional adult actions that prioritize trust, affirmation, and access. These steps focus on what educators and leaders can design and sustain.

1. Build trusted relationships through consistent connection

Establish predictable check-ins that allow students to feel seen and supported. Consistency communicates care more powerfully than isolated gestures and helps students identify adults they can trust.

2. Integrate SEL practices that affirm identity

Use reflective tools such as journaling, art, storytelling, or discussion to help students process emotions and identity in safe, affirming ways. SEL activities should invite expression without requiring disclosure.

3. Ensure access to trained, affirming counseling support

Provide counseling services led by professionals who understand LGBTQIA+ identities, confidentiality, and trauma-informed care. Clear protocols help students seek support without fear. **Resource 8.4: Mental Health Access Guide** clarifies pathways for affirming mental health services. Utilize this tool to build out support services that are available at a moment's notice.

4. Strengthen peer support and community

Support student-led groups such as Gay-Straight Alliances or affinity spaces that reduce isolation and foster belonging. Peer connection reinforces that students are not alone in their experiences.

5. Affirm identity through curriculum and school culture

Incorporate inclusive stories, language, and events throughout the year rather than limiting affirmation to specific moments. To expand representation within the curriculum, **Resource 8.2: LGBTQIA+ Literature List** integrates affirming texts across content areas, reinforcing identity as part of everyday learning.

Reflection Prompts

- How are emotional needs acknowledged and addressed within daily classroom routines?
- Which SEL practices affirm diverse identities rather than assuming uniform experiences?
- How do adults normalize conversations about feelings, stress, and belonging?
- Where might students need discreet pathways to support rather than public ones?

Then What?

In the short term, students demonstrate renewed engagement, improved attendance, and stronger relationships with adults and peers. Teachers notice subtle, but meaningful, indicators of safety returning—eye contact, participation, laughter, or willingness to take academic risks. These moments signal that emotional energy is no longer consumed by fear or isolation.

Over time, schools embed SEL practices into culture rather than relying on individual staff members. Leaders use student feedback, engagement data, and climate indicators to refine support. As well-being becomes a shared responsibility, LGBTQIA+ students experience school as a place where care and learning are inseparable.

What If?

What if students are hesitant to seek support or fear being identified? Discretion and visibility are not opposites—they can coexist. Schools can offer confidential options such as anonymous forms, digital check-ins, or quiet outreach from trusted adults. When students know support is available without pressure or exposure, they are more likely to access help. Over time, consistent care builds the trust that allows students to step forward when they are ready.

Way 31 — Engaging Families and Communities in LGBTQIA+ Inclusion: Extending Belonging Beyond School

What?

This Way recognizes that inclusion deepens when schools extend belonging beyond their walls. For LGBTQIA+ students, affirmation at school can be life-giving—but when families and communities are also engaged, support becomes more durable and protective.

Family engagement invites learning, dialogue, and understanding, while acknowledging that not all home environments are affirming or safe.

Schools play a critical role in bridging this gap. By hosting learning opportunities, sharing trusted resources, and building partnerships with local LGBTQIA+ organizations, schools broaden the circle of care around students. Inclusion becomes not just a classroom value, but a community commitment grounded in dignity and respect.

Why?

Family acceptance is a powerful protective factor. Research from the *Family Acceptance Project* (2022) shows that LGBTQIA+ youth who experience family affirmation are significantly less likely to experience depression, substance use, or suicidal ideation. Even incremental shifts in understanding—from caregivers, extended family, or community adults—can meaningfully improve student well-being.

Consistent, compassionate communication from educators can turn hesitation into empathy over time. When schools partner with community organizations, they amplify resources and model shared responsibility for student safety and belonging. These partnerships also signal to students that their identities are valued not only within school, but within the broader community that surrounds them.

This work aligns directly with social-emotional learning. CASEL (2022) emphasizes that SEL thrives in environments where students experience relationship skills, social awareness, and self-management across settings—not only within classrooms. For LGBTQIA+ students, aligned messages of care and inclusion across school, family, and community strengthen resilience and reinforce emotional safety.

How?

Engaging families and communities in LGBTQIA+ inclusion requires intentional outreach, clarity of purpose, and sustained relationship-building. These steps focus on adult actions that extend affirmation while honoring diverse starting points.

1. Host learning opportunities grounded in care and curiosity

Provide approachable, judgment-free workshops that build understanding of gender identity, sexual orientation, and student well-being. Learning spaces should invite questions, normalize growth, and center student safety rather than debate. Strengthening home–school partnership, **Resource 8.5: Family Partnership Support Tool** equips families with affirming resources and guidance including a family workshop that schools can host.

2. Share trusted, accessible resources

Offer families and caregivers materials from organizations such as GLSEN, PFLAG, and *The Trevor Project*. Providing clear, vetted resources reduces misinformation and gives adults language to support students more effectively.

3. Build partnerships with local LGBTQIA+ organizations

Collaborate with community advocacy and support groups to extend mentoring, counseling, and family education opportunities. Partnerships expand capacity and reinforce that schools are not working alone.

4. Represent diverse families in school communications

Ensure newsletters, websites, and school stories reflect a range of family structures and identities. Visibility communicates belonging and helps normalize diversity for all families.

5. Communicate with care and consistency

Use inclusive language in all correspondence and model respect in tone and messaging. Consistent communication builds trust and reinforces that inclusion is a shared value.

Reflection Prompts

- How can families learn alongside educators about LGBTQIA+ inclusion and well-being?
- Which community partners could expand our support network for students and caregivers?
- How do our communications model empathy, dignity, and affirmation?
- Where might families need multiple entry points to feel safe engaging with the school?

Then What?

In the short term, schools evaluate participation, feedback, and family questions to refine engagement strategies. Stories of evolving understanding—rather than immediate agreement—become indicators of progress. Students benefit from knowing that adults are learning and growing alongside them.

Over time, family and community engagement strengthens student resilience and connection. Supporting this growth, **Resource 8.3: SEL Activity Collection** provides structured opportunities to build social-emotional skills such as relationship-building, empathy, and self-awareness. As alignment deepens across school, home, and community, LGBTQIA+ students experience more consistent affirmation and emotional safety.

What If?

What if families resist or disengage? Resistance often reflects fear or lack of information rather than rejection. Schools can keep doors open, continue modeling empathy, and avoid positioning engagement as all-or-nothing. For students who lack affirmation at home, strengthening networks of caring adults within school becomes even more essential. When schools lead with patience and clarity, inclusion grows steadily—even when the path is uneven.

Way 32 — Empowering LGBTQIA+ Students Through Peer Mentorship: Belonging Built Side by Side

What?

This Way positions peer mentorship as a powerful strategy for transforming isolation into belonging. For LGBTQIA+ students, connection with peers who share similar experiences—or who are committed allies—can provide affirmation that feels immediate, credible, and deeply personal. Peer mentorship pairs younger students or those seeking connection with trained mentors who offer support, perspective, and encouragement.

Peer mentorship does not replace adult support; it complements it. When students see themselves reflected in one another, they experience school as a place where they are not alone. This Way emphasizes mentorship structures that honor identity, build leadership, and create networks of care that strengthen school culture from within.

Why?

Role models play a critical role in shaping students' sense of belonging and possibility. Research by Toomey and Russell (2023) demonstrates that peer mentorship reduces stigma, increases feelings of belonging, and supports academic persistence for LGBTQIA+ students. Mentorship also benefits mentors themselves, fostering leadership skills, empathy, and a deeper sense of purpose.

Without intentional peer connection, LGBTQIA+ students may navigate school feeling unseen or isolated, even in otherwise supportive environments. Peer mentorship interrupts this pattern by normalizing experience and reinforcing that identity is not a barrier to success. When students support one another within structured, caring systems, confidence grows—and so does engagement.

How?

Empowering LGBTQIA+ students through peer mentorship requires thoughtful design, clear expectations, and ongoing reflection. These steps focus on adult-created structures that allow student leadership and connection to flourish safely.

1. Create structured, voluntary mentorship programs

Design mentorship opportunities with clear goals, expectations, and boundaries. Participation should always be voluntary, allowing students to opt in when they feel ready. Structure ensures safety while supporting authentic connection. Fostering peer connection, **Resource 8.6: Peer Mentorship Framework** creates structured opportunities for student-to-student support.

2. Prepare mentors with intentional training

Equip mentors with active listening skills, identity awareness, confidentiality expectations, and clear referral pathways to adult support. Training ensures mentors feel confident and supported rather than overburdened.

3. Foster community through shared reflection and celebration

Provide opportunities for mentors and mentees to reflect together and celebrate growth. Community gatherings reinforce connection and help students see mentorship as part of a broader culture of belonging.

4. Amplify student voice through co-design

Invite students to help shape mentorship activities, norms, and focus areas. Co-design reinforces agency and ensures the program reflects students' lived realities rather than adult assumptions.

5. Evaluate and sustain through ongoing feedback

Use student feedback, reflection, and participation data to refine the program annually. Continuous improvement ensures mentorship remains responsive, relevant, and meaningful.

Reflection Prompts

- How does peer mentorship honor both identity and leadership for LGBTQIA+ students?
- What training and support do mentors need to sustain healthy relationships?
- How might peer mentorship influence the broader culture of belonging in our school?
- Where do students need choice or discretion within mentorship structures?

Then What?

In the short term, students report increased confidence, connection, and willingness to engage in school life. Educators notice stronger peer relationships, improved attendance, and reduced isolation among students who participate. Success is measured not only in outcomes, but in stories of growth, trust, and emerging leadership.

Over time, peer mentorship becomes a visible expression of school values. As mentors develop leadership skills and mentees build confidence, mentorship ripples outward—shaping peer norms, strengthening allyship, and reinforcing a culture where students look out for one another. Schools track both mentor and mentee growth to ensure the program continues to support student well-being and academic persistence.

What If?

What if students fear visibility or worry about being identified through participation? Safety and choice must remain central. Schools can offer anonymous sign-ups, hybrid or small-group options, and flexible participation models that protect privacy. Empowerment does not always begin publicly. When schools honor discretion alongside connection, more students are willing to engage—on their own terms and in their own time.

Closing Reflection

Months later, Lucas no longer waits for the room to empty before he speaks. He raises his hand without hesitation. He volunteers to read passages aloud. He joined the student advisory council and helped organize a display for Pride Month that featured authors and historical figures he once only researched quietly on his own. His writing—once guarded and coded—now carries clarity and conviction. Where there was once careful distance, there is now presence. Not performative. Not loud. Just fully himself.

Being seen did not change who Lucas was. It changed how safe he felt being who he already was. And that safety translated into confidence, engagement, and academic growth. When we create environments where students do not have to edit themselves to belong, we free up their energy for learning, leadership, and joy. Lucas didn't need to be fixed. He needed to be affirmed. Once he was heard, he didn't just participate—he flourished. There is no singular roadmap to supporting LGBTQIA+ students. Each journey is personal. But one constant remains: schools can be sanctuaries. We may not control the world beyond our walls, but we control how students are treated at 8:05 a.m. when the bell rings.

Every inclusive act—every chosen name honored, every slur interrupted, every story represented—builds a culture in which learning and love coexist. The test of our leadership isn't how we treat those who fit the mold, but how we embrace those who challenge it.

The Constellation of Learning™ Synopsis

This chapter shines through **Student-Centered Culture & Engagement**, inviting educators to build schools where LGBTQIA+ students can live authentically and learn unapologetically. Engagement emerges when identity is safe to exist in daylight—where policies affirm, pronouns are honored, and classrooms echo inclusion in every word and wall.

Culture under this constellation is not performative; it's protective. It asks us to transform allyship into action and affirmation into architecture. When belonging is built into the blueprint, students stop hiding and start thriving.

Hallway Confessions – Daily Practice and Perspective

"Not every student is going to share their story," one school leader reflected. *"That's why we have to lead with compassion instead of assumptions."* They went on to explain that authentic visibility matters far more than performative gestures—students notice when care is real. When support is normalized through everyday practices like consistent pronoun respect, safety stops feeling exceptional and starts feeling expected. *"The work has to be proactive,"* she added. *"We build safety rituals before harm ever happens."* In the end, she reminded us that every interaction, every poster on a wall, and every pronoun used in a hallway conversation becomes a choice point—either affirming a student's identity or quietly eroding it. Choose affirmation.

The Dismissal Bell – The Five A's

When the final bell rings, we must ask whether LGBTQIA+ students leave school affirmed—or exhausted from hiding. Belonging cannot be conditional on silence, neutrality, or compliance. For too many students, safety is negotiated moment by moment, shaped by language, policies, and whether adults choose to intervene or look away. When schools move from tolerance to affirmation, identity no longer feels risky and learning no longer requires self-erasure. Equity is realized when every student leaves knowing they are safe, seen, and valued—not in spite of who they are, but because of it.

Action Step	Description
Audit	Examine classrooms and policies. Where is representation missing?
Adjust	Make one visible change this week that signals inclusion.
Advocate	Speak up for students who cannot yet speak for themselves.
Assemble	Collaborate across teams to embed inclusivity schoolwide.
Attitude Ask	Do you believe every student deserves to feel safe, validated, and empowered? What visible evidence of inclusion exists in my classroom today? How do my daily choices communicate belonging? What will I do tomorrow to make safety unmistakable?

CHAPTER 9

High-Ability Students: Empowering Potential Beyond the Ceiling

Opening Vignette

Marcus sat in the back corner of his fifth-grade classroom, quietly sketching detailed architectural blueprints on the back of his math worksheet. His teacher, focused on helping struggling students master fractions, often praised Marcus for being "easy." He finished his work quickly, rarely caused disruption, and smiled when asked to help peers. What his teacher didn't see was the growing boredom behind that polite grin. Marcus had learned to hide his curiosity—to keep his endless "what-if" questions to himself so he wouldn't stand out. His brilliance didn't need remediation, so it went largely unnoticed. By spring, his enthusiasm for learning had faded to compliance.

Stories like Marcus's are repeated in classrooms everywhere. High-ability students—those with exceptional intellectual, creative, or leadership potential—are often assumed to be fine without targeted support. Yet unchallenged talent can erode just as surely as unmet need. When we neglect to nurture these learners, we risk losing the very innovation, empathy, and leadership our schools and communities most need.

Framing the Challenge

High-ability students represent approximately 6–10 percent of the U.S. K–12 population (U.S. Department of Education, 2023), but the percentage of students identified as gifted varies dramatically by state and demographic. According to the National Center for Research on Gifted Education (2022), students from low-income backgrounds are underrepresented by as much as fifty percent in gifted programs, and Black, Hispanic, and Native American students remain significantly less likely to be identified compared with white and Asian peers. Moreover, bilingual and twice-exceptional learners (those who are both gifted and have a disability) are frequently misidentified or overlooked altogether (Missett et al., 2023).

The challenge is not simply one of access to gifted programs—it's a matter of equity, opportunity, and mindset. Too often, giftedness is conflated with privilege or early academic success, when in truth it reflects potential that may be masked by circumstance. A truly student-centered system identifies and nurtures ability in every context, not only in those already advantaged by resources or advocacy.

Between 2022 and 2025, more than a dozen states revised their gifted-education regulations to require universal screening or local-norm identification models, a promising trend toward inclusion (NAGC, 2024). Yet many districts still lack the staffing, training, and culturally responsive tools necessary to implement those mandates effectively. Without systemic change, the result is predictable: a widening excellence gap where high-potential students from marginalized communities rarely see their gifts recognized—or see them fade from disuse.

High-ability learners need educators who move beyond "more of the same." They need complexity, creativity, and connection. They need adults who will see in them what others might overlook—and who will design learning experiences that make brilliance feel like belonging.

Way 33 — Differentiate Beyond Enrichment: Designing for Depth, Not More

What?

This Way reframes differentiation for high-ability students as a matter of design rather than volume. High-ability learners do not need simply *more* work; they need *different* work—work that invites depth, complexity, and intellectual risk. Differentiation begins with intentional curriculum design that allows for flexible pacing, independent inquiry, and opportunities for creative synthesis.

True differentiation moves beyond enrichment as an add-on. It creates learning pathways where students can engage deeply with ideas, explore multiple perspectives, and construct meaning in sophisticated ways. When instruction is designed for depth, high-ability students experience challenge without isolation and rigor without redundancy.

Why?

Research consistently shows that many high-ability students spend significant portions of the school day engaged in content they have already mastered. Reis and Renzulli (2022) found that advanced learners may spend up to forty percent of classroom time on previously learned material. Over time, this stagnation can lead to disengagement, underachievement, and behaviors often misinterpreted as lack of motivation.

Thoughtful differentiation restores challenge and purpose. When instruction honors readiness and intellectual pace, students re-engage with learning and develop habits of inquiry, persistence, and creativity. Importantly, this work reinforces equity by ensuring that every learner—regardless of starting point—is expected to grow. Differentiation is not about privilege; it is about responsibility to meet students where they are.

How?

Differentiating beyond enrichment requires proactive planning and responsive instructional choices. These steps focus on adult design decisions that create space for advanced learning without fragmenting the classroom community.

1. Pre-assess learning and compact curriculum intentionally

Use pre-assessment to identify prior mastery, then remove redundant instruction. Curriculum compacting frees time for advanced learning experiences without accelerating students through content prematurely.

2. Offer meaningful choice and voice in learning pathways

Design open-ended tasks that allow for multiple solutions, products, or modalities. Choice increases ownership and allows students to demonstrate understanding in ways that reflect their interests and strengths.

3. Anchor learning in real-world and interdisciplinary application

Connect projects to authentic community issues or interdisciplinary problems. Real-world application increases relevance and invites students to apply knowledge across contexts rather than in isolation.

4. Increase cognitive demand through depth and complexity

Use tools such as Kaplan's depth and complexity prompts—language of the discipline, big ideas, rules, patterns, trends, ethics, and perspectives—to deepen thinking. These prompts elevate rigor without increasing workload.

To honor readiness and intellectual pace, **Resource 9.1: Depth, Complexity & Curriculum Compacting Planner** supports responsive instructional design that maintains challenge while preserving coherence.

Reflection Prompts

+ How often do extension activities deepen thinking rather than simply extend time on task?
+ Which students might benefit from curriculum compacting or independent learning pathways?
+ Where could depth and complexity prompts replace additional assignments?
+ How does differentiation reinforce growth for all learners in the classroom?

Then What?

In the short term, high-ability students demonstrate renewed engagement, persistence, and curiosity. Teachers observe more sophisticated questions, higher-quality products, and increased willingness to take intellectual risks. Growth is documented through qualitative measures such as student reflections, performance rubrics, and portfolio artifacts.

Over time, differentiation becomes a shared instructional stance rather than an individual accommodation. Teams refine practices, calibrate expectations, and expand opportunities for advanced inquiry. The goal is not faster completion of work, but richer cognition and deeper learning experiences that challenge every student appropriately.

What If?

What if enrichment became the norm rather than the exception? Classrooms would shift from coverage to curiosity, and learning would be defined by depth rather than pace. When differentiation is embedded into design, "gifted" describes a learning experience—not a label. Students of all readiness levels benefit from environments that value complexity, creativity, and meaningful challenge.

Way 34 — Honoring the Whole Learner: Excellence With Emotional Grounding

What?

This Way reframes how schools understand and support high-ability students by recognizing them as whole learners—not just high performers. While these students often demonstrate advanced cognitive skills, many simultaneously navigate perfectionism, social isolation, or asynchronous development, where emotional maturity lags behind intellectual ability. Honoring the whole learner means addressing social-emotional and identity needs with the same intentionality used to support academic growth.

High-ability students benefit from environments that acknowledge complexity rather than reward performance alone. When schools attend to well-being alongside challenge, students experience learning as sustainable rather than exhausting. This Way emphasizes balance—cultivating intellectual rigor while supporting emotional resilience, self-awareness, and belonging.

Why?

Research indicates that high-ability learners are not immune to stress or self-doubt. Neihart and Betts (2023) report that up to one-third of gifted adolescents experience anxiety or feelings of impostorism when comparing themselves to peers. In environments where achievement is emphasized without attention to well-being, students may internalize the belief that their value is tied solely to performance.

Supporting social-emotional growth sustains long-term excellence. When students develop self-regulation, empathy, and resilience, they are better equipped to navigate challenges, recover from setbacks, and maintain motivation. Addressing these needs is not a departure from rigor; it is a prerequisite for enduring creativity and achievement. Often overlooked in advanced learning spaces, **Resource 9.2: High-Ability Learner SEL & Identity Guide** addresses the social-emotional and identity dimensions essential to holistic growth.

How?

Honoring the whole learner requires adult actions that normalize humanity alongside high expectations. These steps focus on instructional and relational design choices that support both mind and heart.

1. Model vulnerability and the learning process

Share stories of struggle, revision, and growth to normalize imperfection. When adults model learning as iterative, students learn that excellence includes reflection and recovery—not just correctness.

2. Integrate SEL practices with academic challenge

Pair rigorous tasks with structured reflection on effort, emotion, and perseverance. Integrating SEL within challenge helps students develop awareness of how they respond to complexity and stress.

3. Create affinity spaces for connection and support

Facilitate peer groups, mentorships, or discussion spaces where high-ability students can connect without stigma. Affinity spaces reduce isolation and provide opportunities for shared understanding and encouragement.

4. Partner with families to reinforce balance

Communicate with families that giftedness does not guarantee confidence or emotional ease. Invite families to reinforce balance, self-care, and healthy expectations at home, aligning messages across environments.

Reflection Prompts

- When do I celebrate curiosity, risk-taking, or persistence rather than correctness alone?
- How am I making it safe for advanced learners to struggle, revise, and fail forward?
- What signals do students receive about the relationship between worth and performance?
- Where might emotional support be needed alongside academic challenge?

Then What?

In the short term, students demonstrate greater willingness to take intellectual risks and engage in challenging work without fear of failure. Educators notice increased reflection, healthier responses to feedback, and stronger peer relationships. Well-being check-ins become a natural companion to academic conferencing.

Over time, schools track not only grades and performance but also indicators of joy, engagement, and belonging. By embedding emotional support into advanced learning structures, schools cultivate learners who sustain creativity, curiosity, and resilience beyond the classroom.

What If?

What if giftedness were reframed as human potential in progress rather than a fixed identity? Learning environments would prioritize growth over comparison and development over perfection.

When schools honor the whole learner, they nurture minds and hearts capable of sustaining excellence, empathy, and innovation long after formal schooling ends.

Way 35 — Designing Systems That See Every Spark: Equity Through Intentional Identification

What?

This Way reframes equity for high-ability students as a systems-design responsibility rather than an individual referral decision. Equity does not begin when students enter gifted programming; it begins with how schools define, look for, and recognize potential. Identification systems that rely primarily on teacher referrals or single standardized measures often privilege students with access, advocacy, or familiarity with dominant cultural norms.

Designing systems that see every spark requires schools to broaden their understanding of giftedness and intentionally remove barriers embedded in traditional identification practices. Universal screening, multiple criteria, and local-norm benchmarks shift the question from *"Who fits the program?"* to *"How do we recognize potential wherever it exists?"* When systems are designed with equity in mind, opportunity expands without lowering standards.

To support this systems-level shift, **Resource 9.3: Gifted Identification & Talent Development Tool** introduces the OPEN Framework for High-Ability Identification and Talent Development. Rather than treating gifted identification as a one-time event or gatekeeping process, the OPEN Framework positions talent as something to be intentionally located, nurtured, and expanded over time. OPEN—Opportunity, Pathways, Equity, and Nurture— provides schools with a coherent, equity-centered approach for designing identification systems that surface potential across contexts, not just among students with early access or advocacy. By focusing on opportunity before labels and development before placement, the framework helps districts move from asking who qualifies to examining how systems are designed to see every spark.

Why?

Research demonstrates that identification practices shape who is seen—and who is overlooked. Card and Giuliano (2023) found that districts implementing universal screening significantly increased identification of historically underrepresented students, with Black and Hispanic student representation increasing by more than one hundred eighty percent compared to traditional referral-based models. These findings underscore a critical truth: talent does not change—systems do.

When gifted programs more closely reflect the demographics of the district, schools send a powerful message about belonging and expectation. Students begin to see advanced learning as attainable rather than exclusive. Systemic design matters because it determines whose brilliance is recognized early and whose potential may remain untapped.

How?

Designing equitable identification systems requires intentional choices, transparency, and sustained monitoring. These steps focus on adult decisions that reshape access to opportunity.

1. Implement universal screening at multiple grade levels

Assess all students using developmentally appropriate, culturally responsive measures rather than relying on referrals. Universal screening reduces bias and ensures that potential is not dependent on advocacy or visibility.

2. Apply local norms to identify potential within context
Compare students to peers within the same school rather than national averages. Local norms help surface talent that may otherwise be obscured by systemic inequities tied to opportunity and access.

3. Broaden definitions of giftedness through professional learning
Invest in training that helps educators recognize diverse manifestations of giftedness, including creativity, leadership, linguistic ability, spatial reasoning, and problem-solving. Broad definitions increase the likelihood that all forms of brilliance are valued.

4. Monitor and share equity data with transparency
Regularly review and publish identification and placement data disaggregated by race, language, gender, and socioeconomic status. Transparency builds accountability and keeps equity at the center of decision-making.

Reflection Prompts
- Does our current identification process prioritize access or advantage?
- Which students or communities may still be underrepresented—and why?
- How do our definitions of giftedness reflect cultural values and assumptions?
- In what ways are data conversations leading to action rather than compliance?

Then What?
In the short term, schools engage in courageous data conversations that examine patterns, assumptions, and outcomes. Teams use data not as a compliance exercise, but as a catalyst for reflection

and redesign. Early changes in identification practices begin to shift who is seen and supported.

Over time, equitable identification becomes embedded in district culture. Criteria are reviewed regularly, outcomes are monitored transparently, and student stories are considered alongside metrics. As systems evolve, more students experience advanced learning as an expectation rather than an exception.

What If?

What if identification became a doorway rather than a gate? Leaders would stop asking who qualifies and start asking which systems need redesign. When schools commit to examining data, revisiting criteria, and widening how they define potential, students across neighborhoods, backgrounds, and identities receive the same message: brilliance is expected—everywhere.

Way 36 — Connecting Communities to Cultivate Potential: Purpose Beyond the Classroom

What?

This Way positions community connection as an essential lever for cultivating high-ability potential. Advanced learning thrives when schools partner with families, businesses, universities, and community organizations to extend learning beyond classroom walls. Authentic mentorships, internships, research experiences, and service projects give high-ability students context, purpose, and humility—transforming talent into contribution.

Connecting communities to learning reframes giftedness as a responsibility rather than a status. When students apply advanced skills to real needs, they deepen understanding while developing empathy, collaboration, and civic awareness. This Way emphasizes learning that is rooted in place and purpose, ensuring that high-ability development serves both the learner and the community.

Why?

Research shows that when advanced learners engage in real-world problem-solving, motivation and persistence increase significantly. Siegle et al. (2024) note that authentic partnerships strengthen engagement by providing relevance and challenge that traditional classroom tasks often cannot replicate. These experiences help students see the impact of their work and the value of sustained effort.

Community-connected learning also counters elitism by grounding gifted programs in service and collaboration. When high-ability students work alongside community members, they learn that leadership is relational and that expertise grows through listening as much as through performance. Partnerships reinforce that gifted education is not about separation, but about meaningful contribution.

How?

Connecting communities to cultivate potential requires intentional design and coordination. These steps focus on adult actions that expand opportunity while maintaining coherence and equity.

1. Create mentorship networks aligned to student interests
Pair students with community experts in STEM, the arts, entrepreneurship, or leadership. Mentorship provides guidance, real-world insight, and role modeling while helping students envision pathways beyond school.

2. Leverage local universities and institutions
Establish early-college courses, summer research opportunities, or lab partnerships that allow students to engage in advanced study.

These experiences deepen content knowledge and introduce students to academic and professional cultures.

3. Design passion projects with community benefit

Invite students to pursue projects connected to authentic issues that matter to others. Passion projects that serve real needs foster ownership, creativity, and a sense of responsibility.

4. Highlight civic impact as a measure of success

Publicly recognize how advanced learning contributes to community growth. Showcasing impact reinforces that giftedness is measured not only by achievement, but by how learning improves lives.

To connect learning with purpose, **Resource 9.4: Community Mentorship & Passion Project Playbook** supports schools in designing, sustaining, and evaluating community partnerships that expand opportunity.

Reflection Prompts

- Do our partnerships expand opportunity, or do they inadvertently reinforce privilege?
- How are students supported in connecting advanced learning to service and impact?
- Which community voices are included—and which are missing—in partnership design?
- How do these experiences shape students' understanding of leadership?

Then What?

In the short term, students develop impact portfolios that document learning through contribution—artifacts, reflections, and outcomes that demonstrate how their work benefits others. Educators and leaders share these portfolios with families and boards to illustrate that gifted education is, at its core, community education.

Over time, partnerships deepen and diversify. Schools refine systems for access, coordination, and reflection so that community-connected learning becomes a sustained pathway rather than a one-time experience. As alignment grows, students experience advanced learning as purposeful, connected, and responsive to the world around them.

What If?

What if gifted programs measured success by contribution rather than competition? Leaders would design partnerships that prioritize service, reflection, and shared problem-solving. When schools commit to cultivating potential through community connection, they raise innovators who lead with empathy—and use their abilities in service of others.

Closing Reflection

When we picture equity, we often think of raising the floor. Yet equity also means lifting the ceiling. High-ability students remind us that potential exists in every zip code, waiting for adults willing to design learning that challenges as much as it cares.

When we picture equity, we often think of raising the floor. Yet equity also means lifting the ceiling.

Marcus—the boy from our opening vignette—found a mentor the next year who noticed his drawings. With support, he joined a community architecture club, presented designs at a local fair, and rediscovered the joy of learning that comes from being *seen*.

Creating conditions where brilliance belongs is not about gifted programs alone; it's about school cultures that assume every student has gifts worth finding. When we see giftedness as possibility, not privilege, we fulfill the promise that *all means all*—and that excellence and equity can rise together.

The Constellation of Learning™ Synopsis

The theme of **Human-Centered Innovation** defines this chapter, reminding us that high-ability students require more than enrichment—they require empathy. Innovation begins when we see giftedness not as privilege but as a call to personalize learning for those who crave depth, challenge, and connection.

This constellation pushes us to innovate beyond acceleration and toward authenticity. By designing experiences that foster curiosity, collaboration, and creative risk-taking, we cultivate both intellect and humility. Innovation, when human-centered, ensures brilliance never outpaces belonging.

Hallway Confessions – Daily Practice and Perspective

We once sat in a middle-school hallway after a PD session when a teacher sighed, "I'd love to challenge my gifted kids, but I can barely reach the rest." It wasn't cynicism—it was exhaustion. The misconception that supporting advanced learners takes away from others keeps us trapped in a false dichotomy.

Gifted students aren't asking for *more* attention—they're asking for *appropriate* attention. It's the same request we honor for every learner. The truth is that when we differentiate for high-ability students, we sharpen practices for all: pre-assessing, flexible grouping, and designing tasks with multiple entry points.

The next time you hear "They'll be fine on their own," pause. Fine is not the goal. Flourishing is.

The Dismissal Bell – The Five A's

When the final bell rings, the question is not who excelled—but who was quietly waiting. High-ability students often leave school having completed the work but never entered the learning. Potential does not always announce itself; it hides in early finishers, compliant behavior, and unasked questions. When schools design systems that look beyond speed and scores, they turn unnoticed aptitude into sustained growth. By challenging, nurturing, and expanding opportunity, we transform quiet compliance into curiosity—and ensure brilliance is not just recognized, but developed.

Action Step	Description
Audit	Examine who has access to advanced coursework, enrichment, and mentorship.
Adjust	Replace barriers with bridges—multiple entry points for students to demonstrate potential.
Advocate	Use data and storytelling to promote equitable talent development across grades.
Assemble	Build teams that keep identification transparent and culturally responsive.
Attitude Ask	Choose to see giftedness not as an exception, but as an expectation.

CHAPTER 10

English Learner Students: Language as Bridge, Not Barrier

Opening Vignette

Mrs. Harper used to believe she was helping. She had been teaching seventh-grade English for more than a decade and prided herself on finding ways to make difficult texts "more accessible" for her English Learners. She shortened passages, simplified vocabulary, and gave sentence starters that did most of the cognitive work. Her intentions were kind; she wanted her multilingual students to feel successful. But one afternoon during independent reading, she overheard José quietly tell a classmate, "I don't read the big book anymore—mine's the easy one."

That moment unsettled her. She realized the strategies meant to include José had quietly excluded him from the challenge. Later that week, during a professional-learning session, she heard a colleague say, *"When we lower the language, we lower the thinking."* The statement stayed with her. She began to ask different questions: *What if scaffolding isn't about simplifying? What if it's about unlocking?*

By semester's end, Mrs. Harper stopped editing out complex words and instead built background knowledge, modeled context-clue strategies, and invited students to share translations of key terms in their home languages. The transformation wasn't instantaneous, but she saw confidence growing in ways that worksheets never sparked. As she reflected, she realized the shift wasn't just about instruction—it was about mindset. Supporting English Learners was less about what she removed and more about what she restored: rigor, dignity, and voice.

Framing the Challenge

Across the United States, the number of English Learners (ELs) continues to climb. According to the National Center for Education Statistics (NCES, 2024), more than 5.4 million students—about 10.5 percent of public-school enrollment—were classified as ELs in 2022, an increase of nearly six percent since 2018. The U.S. Department of Education (2023) reports that over four hundred home languages are represented nationwide, with Spanish, Arabic, Chinese, Vietnamese, and Somali among the most common. These learners bring tremendous linguistic and cultural capital to classrooms, yet their academic outcomes often reveal systemic inequities.

National assessment data from 2023 show that EL students scored, on average, 34 points lower in reading and 37 points lower in mathematics on the NAEP than their non-EL peers (NCES, 2024). Graduation rates have improved—from 66 percent in 2015 to 74 percent in 2022—but still trail the national average by more than ten points (U.S. Department of Education, 2023). Compounding the challenge, teacher-preparation programs report limited coursework devoted to linguistically responsive instruction; fewer than 40 percent of U.S. teachers feel confident differentiating for English Learners (WIDA Consortium, 2023).

These data illuminate both urgency and opportunity. When educators view multilingualism as an asset rather than an obstacle, classroom discourse becomes richer, student identity stronger, and academic engagement deeper. Schools that intentionally build structures for co-teaching, family partnership, and professional learning in language development demonstrate higher EL growth trajectories (Sugarman & Geary, 2023).

As we move into the four upcoming Ways 37–40, we'll explore how educators can shift from compliance-driven supports to empowered, asset-based design. The goal is not simply helping students *survive* in English—it's helping them *thrive* through it.

Way 37 — Building Bridges Through Language and Culture

What?

Every English Learner enters school with a story that extends far beyond vocabulary lists and sentence frames. Language is more than communication—it is identity, family, history, and hope. Building bridges through language and culture means intentionally seeing multilingualism not as a barrier to overcome but as a superpower that enhances learning for everyone. When educators intentionally connect instruction to students' cultural and linguistic assets, they transform classrooms from places of translation to spaces of belonging.

The bridge begins with recognition. Every time we invite a student to share a home-language term, celebrate a cultural holiday, or connect curriculum to lived experience, we send a message: *You belong here, and your story matters.* Creating these bridges demands more than celebration—it requires sustained curiosity about who our students are and how language shapes the way they see and navigate the world. Clarifying proficiency vs cognition, **Resource 10.1: EL Proficiency Framework Visual** preserves rigor.

Why?

Research consistently demonstrates that affirming students' linguistic and cultural identities improves academic outcomes and social belonging. García and Kleifgen (2022) note that bilingual learners thrive when schools "position language diversity as a strength to cultivate, not a challenge to remediate" (p. 14). Likewise, the Office of English Language Acquisition (OELA, 2024) found that schools using culturally responsive and asset-based language practices report up to fifteen percent higher reading growth among multilingual learners compared with schools using deficit-framed approaches.

The "why" is rooted in equity. For too long, English Learners have been viewed through a lens of deficiency—students who "lack" English proficiency rather than students who *possess* multiple linguistic systems. Building bridges shifts the narrative from remediation to recognition. It aligns with research on culturally sustaining pedagogy, which argues that academic success must not come at the expense of linguistic and cultural identity (Paris & Alim, 2022). When educators value home languages and incorporate them into daily instruction, they strengthen trust, engagement, and self-efficacy—key predictors of long-term academic growth.

How?

1. Create visibility for language diversity

Display multilingual labels, signs, and greetings throughout classrooms and hallways. Encourage students to contribute phrases from their home languages.

2. Use translanguaging strategies

Allow students to access prior knowledge in their home language before transferring understanding to English.

3. Integrate cultural storytelling

Invite students and families to share stories, music, or traditions connected to curriculum themes.

4. Design lessons that blend content and context

Use visual scaffolds, real-world examples, and culturally relevant texts that affirm student experience.

5. Lead with curiosity, not correction

Ask, "What does this word mean in your language?" instead of "Say it the right way."

Reflection Prompts

- What messages do your classroom materials and routines send about whose languages are valued?
- When students share their cultural backgrounds, how do you respond—curiously or cautiously?
- Which curriculum areas offer the most natural entry points for linguistic and cultural connections?
- How might you use families as co-teachers in building language bridges?

Then What?

Building bridges is not a one-time event—it's a daily stance. Start by mapping the linguistic assets already in your classroom. Identify the languages spoken, the cultural traditions represented, and the stories that remain untold. Then, choose one unit to redesign using those assets as the foundation. Partner with families and bilingual staff to ensure accuracy and authenticity.

What If?

What if every hallway echoed with more than English? What if students heard their own languages affirmed and saw their cultures reflected in the lessons we teach? When we build bridges through language and culture, we don't just help English Learners cross into understanding—we invite all students to walk across together.

Way 38 — From Access to Achievement: Scaffolding with Intention

What?

For English Learners, access is too often treated as the finish line. Lessons are simplified, texts are shortened, and accommodations are checked off as evidence of equity. Scaffolding with intention reframes access as the starting point—not the goal. True scaffolding is not about dilution; it is about design. It preserves cognitive demand while intentionally building pathways for students to engage, express, and extend their thinking.

Scaffolding with intention means planning for how students will enter complex content, not whether they will encounter it at all. It requires educators to distinguish between language proficiency and conceptual understanding and to design instruction that supports both simultaneously. Guiding instructional choice, **Resource 10.2: Instructional Decision Pathway Tool** aligns demand and access, helping educators maintain rigor while removing unnecessary barriers.

Why?

Research is clear that English Learners make the greatest academic gains when language development is embedded within rigorous, content-rich instruction. The National Academies of Sciences, Engineering, and Medicine (2023) report that students progress most when teachers explicitly plan for language objectives alongside grade-level content rather than replacing complexity with simplification.

Zwiers (2020) reinforces this finding, reminding educators that "students acquire academic language through rich interaction with complex ideas, not avoidance of them" (p. 18). When scaffolds replace thinking rather than support it, students remain dependent and disengaged. When scaffolds are intentional and temporary, students build independence, confidence, and academic voice. Equity is not achieved by lowering expectations—it is achieved by designing access to meet them.

How?

Scaffolding with intention requires deliberate instructional planning that anticipates language demands and fades support as students grow. These steps focus on adult decisions that elevate access without compromising rigor.

1. **Plan lessons with parallel content and language objectives**
Write both what students will learn and how they will communicate that learning. Language objectives clarify the vocabulary, sentence structures, and discourse moves students need to engage meaningfully with the content.

2. **Layer supports purposefully and fade them intentionally**
Begin with visual supports, graphic organizers, or sentence frames, then gradually remove them as students demonstrate readiness. Scaffolds should build capacity, not create dependence.

3. **Preteach vocabulary within meaningful context**
Introduce academic terms through visuals, examples, and discussion tied directly to the lesson. Vocabulary instruction should deepen understanding rather than isolate words from ideas.

4. Model cognitive and linguistic thinking aloud

Verbalize your reasoning, language choices, and problem-solving process. Think-alouds make invisible thinking visible and provide students with models for academic discourse.

5. Encourage structured peer scaffolding

Use intentional talk protocols and collaborative structures that promote authentic language use. Peer interaction increases both comprehension and confidence when thoughtfully designed.

Reflection Prompts

- How often do my scaffolds support student thinking rather than replace it?
- Where could supports be intentionally faded to promote independence?
- Which language demands might be limiting access to complex ideas?
- How do my instructional choices signal belief in students' capacity?

Then What?

Begin by selecting one upcoming lesson and explicitly naming both content and language objectives. Ask, *What vocabulary, sentence structures, or discourse moves will students need to demonstrate understanding?* Then design a scaffold that teaches those moves rather than bypassing them.

Over time, teams can analyze student work to identify which scaffolds accelerate independence and which unintentionally limit it. As intentional scaffolding becomes embedded practice, English Learners move from accessing content to owning it—demonstrating deeper understanding, stronger language development, and increased academic confidence.

What If?

What if scaffolding no longer meant lowering expectations but lifting access? Leaders would coach teachers to plan with intention, monitor independence, and treat rigor as non-negotiable. When scaffolding is designed thoughtfully and removed strategically, English Learners do more than decode content—they engage, contribute, and achieve at high levels.

Way 39 — Collaboration That Counts: Co-Teaching for Equity

What?

When an English Learner is on the roster, every educator shares responsibility for their success. Collaboration that counts moves instruction from parallel efforts to shared ownership of outcomes. Co-teaching for equity is not about dividing tasks or alternating control—it is about designing learning together so that content and language development happen simultaneously.

Effective collaboration ensures that English Learners experience coherent instruction rather than fragmented support. When educators plan, teach, and reflect together, students benefit from consistent expectations, aligned strategies, and clear messages about rigor and belonging. Collaboration becomes a structure for equity, not an optional strategy.

Why?

Research consistently shows that integrated service models—where content and language instruction occur side by side—produce stronger academic outcomes for English Learners. Honigsfeld and Dove (2022) found that co-teaching models improve access to grade-level content while accelerating language development through shared instructional responsibility.

Conversely, when EL instruction is siloed, students are more likely to experience gaps in rigor and continuity. Data from the Office of English Language Acquisition (OELA, 2024) indicate that schools relying on pull-out or isolated models report eighteen percent lower reclassification rates than schools using integrated, collaborative approaches. Equity improves when collaboration is embedded into daily practice rather than dependent on individual effort. To guard against well-intentioned dilution, **Resource 10.3: Rigor Preservation Lens** helps teams examine instructional decisions and ensure that scaffolds preserve cognitive demand rather than replace it.

Resource 10.3: Equity & Belonging Reflection Checklist

Focus Area	Reflection Questions
Curriculum Representation	• Do instructional materials reflect Native American peoples as contemporary communities, not only historical groups? • Are Native voices, authors, or perspectives included in ways that honor accuracy and sovereignty?
Classroom Environment	• Do classroom visuals and displays avoid stereotypes and instead affirm authentic Native identities? • Are land acknowledgments, symbols, or references used thoughtfully rather than decoratively?
Instructional Practices	• Do learning experiences honor multiple ways of knowing, including storytelling, observation, and relational learning? • Are students able to demonstrate understanding through varied formats beyond traditional written responses?

Focus Area	Reflection Questions
Student Voice	• Do Native American students have opportunities to lead, contribute, or share perspectives by choice—not expectation? • Are student contributions affirmed without positioning students as representatives for an entire culture?
Family & Community Connection	• Are tribal families and communities viewed as partners with expertise, not just participants? • Are communication and engagement practices respectful of tribal sovereignty, traditions, and boundaries?

How?

Collaboration that counts requires intentional planning, clarity of roles, and shared reflection. These steps focus on adult actions that strengthen coherence and preserve rigor.

1. Plan together with protected time

Schedule regular co-planning sessions to design lessons that align content objectives with language goals. Planning together ensures that scaffolds, assessments, and expectations are coherent rather than conflicting.

2. Teach together using intentional co-teaching models

Rotate roles strategically using models such as team teaching, station teaching, or parallel instruction. Both educators remain instructional leaders, reinforcing shared authority and accountability. To support intentional design, **Resource 10.4: Scaffold Strategy Menu** provides a range of aligned supports that help educators match scaffolds to identified language demands without lowering expectations.

3. Embed language goals into content instruction

Explicitly identify the vocabulary, discourse patterns, and language structures students need to engage with complex ideas. Language development is planned, not incidental.

4. Reflect together to refine practice

Use brief, focused debriefs to examine what worked, what didn't, and what needs adjustment. Reflection sustains growth and prevents collaboration from becoming performative.

5. Share data to drive timely support

Review formative assessments, student work, and observation notes together. Transparency allows teams to respond quickly while maintaining high expectations.

Reflection Prompts

- How often do we plan instruction together rather than simply share materials?
- Do students experience both educators as equal instructional leaders?
- Where might collaboration strengthen rigor rather than unintentionally reduce it?
- How do our shared decisions reflect belief in students' capacity?

Then What?

Begin by auditing your current EL service model. Identify where instruction is parallel rather than integrated and select one unit to pilot a co-taught approach. Use a simple reflection protocol after implementation: *What did we plan? What did students achieve? What should we adjust next?*

Over time, teams establish norms for shared planning, instruction, and reflection. As collaboration becomes routine, students experience greater coherence, higher expectations, and more consistent access to rigorous learning. Equity moves from intention to structure.

What If?

What if every English Learner saw two educators modeling collaboration and shared accountability? Leaders would protect planning time, clarify roles, and hold teams responsible for collective outcomes. When collaboration counts, equity is no longer a slogan—it is built into how teaching and learning happen every day.

Way 40 — Engaging Families and Communities as Language Partners

What?

This Way reframes family engagement by positioning multilingual families as co-educators rather than recipients of translation. True partnership recognizes that families hold deep expertise about language development, cultural practices, and how children learn best at home. When schools engage families as language partners, they extend learning beyond the classroom and strengthen students' sense of identity and belonging.

Engaging families as language partners requires moving beyond one-way communication toward reciprocal relationships. It means designing systems that invite families into learning—not just logistics—and honoring home languages as assets that support academic growth. When schools treat multilingualism as shared capital, language development becomes a collective responsibility.

Why?

Research confirms that meaningful multilingual family engagement accelerates student success. Sugarman and Geary (2023) found that schools with strong multilingual engagement programs experienced a twenty percent increase in reclassification rates for English Learners. Similarly, Henderson et al. (2022) documented gains in attendance and homework completion when families were encouraged to support learning in students' home languages.

The impact extends beyond academics. When families feel respected as partners, trust deepens and communication improves. Students benefit from consistent messages about the value of language, culture, and effort—reinforcing confidence and motivation. Engaging families as language partners strengthens both instructional coherence and community connection.

How?

Engaging families and communities as language partners requires intentional structures that promote reciprocity, access, and shared learning. These steps focus on adult design decisions that elevate family voice.

1. Establish two-way multilingual communication systems

Ensure communication flows in both directions through translated materials, multilingual platforms, and opportunities for families to respond, ask questions, and offer insights. Partnership begins with listening.

2. Host dialogue-based cultural exchange events

Design events that center on conversation rather than presentation. Invite families to share language practices, stories, and learning strategies connected to classroom goals.

3. Develop Family Language Ambassador roles

Invite bilingual family members to serve as cultural and linguistic bridges—supporting events, welcoming new families, and advising on communication practices.

4. Guarantee consistent interpreter access

Provide trained interpreters for conferences, meetings, and workshops so families can engage fully in academic conversations without language barriers.

5. Offer parent workshops focused on learning, not logistics

Shift workshops from procedural information to instructional partnership—sharing how literacy, language, and content learning can be supported at home in any language.

Community Snapshot

What partnership looks like in practice.

At Lincoln Elementary, Language Lab Night invited families to co-teach literacy games using English and home languages. Families rotated through stations led by students and teachers, strengthening skills while building connection. The result was increased family participation and a shared sense of ownership over learning.

Reflection Prompts

- How are multilingual families positioned as experts in our school community?
- Which communication practices invite partnership—and which may unintentionally exclude?
- How do our engagement structures honor home languages as instructional assets?
- Where could families' insights deepen our understanding of student learning?

Then What?

Begin by mapping current communication patterns to identify whose voices are heard most often—and whose are missing. Invite a small family design group to co-create engagement strategies aligned to learning goals. Make language visible by creating a

"Language Tree" or similar display that celebrates every language spoken in the school.

Over time, schools develop routines that normalize family partnership in instructional conversations. As trust grows, families contribute insights that inform teaching, and students experience stronger alignment between home and school—accelerating language development and academic confidence.

What If?

What if every family conference began with the question, *"Tell me how your child learns best in your home language?"* Leaders would design systems that honor linguistic expertise and invite families into shared problem-solving. When families become true language partners, students inherit not only stronger skills—but pride, connection, and possibility.

Closing Reflection

Mrs. Harper's shift was not a change in care—it was a change in clarity. She did not stop supporting José; she stopped shrinking the work. In doing so, she restored what English Learners too often lose in the name of access: challenge, dignity, and voice. Her classroom became a place where language was no longer a signal of limitation, but a bridge to deeper thinking.

The four Ways in this chapter ask educators to make that same shift. Building bridges through language and culture, scaffolding with intention, collaborating as co-teachers, and engaging families as language partners all point to a shared truth: English Learners do not need less from us—they need better design.

Belonging is not created by simplifying the text. It is created when we refuse to simplify the learner. Language shapes how students experience school, how they understand themselves, and how they connect to the world around them. When educators shift from viewing language as an obstacle to recognizing it as an asset, new pathways for learning emerge. Language is not a wall to climb—it's a window through which students can see the world and themselves.

> Language is not a wall to climb—it's a window through which students can see the world and themselves.

The Constellation of Learning™ Synopsis

This chapter connects to **Instructional Coherence & High-Quality Teaching**, focusing on how English Learners thrive when instruction honors both language and learning. Coherence means clarity—clear goals, scaffolds, and pathways that make rigorous content accessible without diluting meaning.

When educators plan with intention, language becomes the vehicle for empowerment. Instructional coherence is not about simplification; it's about amplification—of vocabulary, voice, and vision. When English Learners are given linguistic dignity, they find academic freedom.

Hallway Confessions – Daily Practice & Perspective

We've all been there—standing at the door as students arrive, hoping our pronunciation of their name is close enough. Or hovering by a parent-teacher conference table, rehearsing the one Spanish phrase we know while praying it comes out right. These moments aren't failures. They're reminders that courage and connection live in the same space.

One teacher shared how she used to rely on Google Translate for every communication. "At first, I was embarrassed," she admitted. "Then I realized my effort mattered more than my accent." Each attempt, no matter how imperfect, told her students: *I see you.*

Another teacher recalled a breakthrough moment when she invited a bilingual student to translate morning directions for the class. "He stood taller that day," she said. "It wasn't just translation—it was leadership."

Hallways are filled with small opportunities to affirm language identity. Greeting students in their home language, learning a new phrase each week, or posting multilingual signs turns routine moments into reminders of belonging. These gestures cost nothing but mean everything.

Of course, there are missteps—mixing up words, pausing mid-sentence—but those vulnerabilities model bravery. They teach students that learning another language is not about perfection; it's about participation. In every imperfect word we speak, we echo a larger truth: language is connection, and connection is the foundation of learning.

The Dismissal Bell – The Five A's

When the final bell rings, we must ask whose voices were heard—and whose were held back by language. English Learners often leave school having understood more than they were allowed to show. Language is not a measure of intelligence, but too often it becomes a gatekeeper to opportunity. When educators design access without lowering expectations, they turn classrooms into places where meaning comes before mastery and dignity comes before fluency. By honoring language as an asset and rigor as nonnegotiable, we ensure students do not leave smaller than they arrived—but stronger, prouder, and more visible.

Action Step	Description
Audit	Identify scaffolds that act as ceilings. Look closely at materials and assignments—are they helping students reach rigor, or are they quietly lowering expectations? Examine lesson plans, feedback, and grouping patterns through a language-equity lens.
Adjust	Embed language goals in every unit. Align content objectives with linguistic outcomes so that speaking, listening, reading, and writing are intentionally cultivated. Adjustment isn't rewriting curriculum—it's rewiring how we measure growth.
Advocate	Spotlight multilingual success. Share stories of progress in newsletters, faculty meetings, and assemblies. When students see their languages and cultures honored publicly, achievement and confidence rise together.
Assemble	Collaborate with families and peers. Build small, consistent teams—teachers, EL specialists, counselors, and parents—who meet to celebrate growth and co-design next steps. Sustainable improvement is always a collective act.
Attitude Ask	What hidden beliefs about language need rewriting? Reflect on assumptions about intelligence, fluency, or "good English." Every belief we rewrite widens access and amplifies belonging.

CHAPTER 11

General Education Students: Illuminating the Invisible Middle

Opening Vignette

Evan sat in the third row, always early but rarely first to speak. His binder was neat, his handwriting careful, and his grades hovered comfortably in the "B" range. Teachers often said, "Evan's fine—he doesn't need much." And so, for years, he floated—never failing, never excelling, just *there*.

During parent-teacher conferences, his mother smiled politely when she heard the familiar refrain: *"Evan's doing just fine."* No one meant harm; "fine" was reassurance. But fine also meant invisible.

In a class buzzing with interventions and extensions, Evan became the quiet center that drew no notice. He completed assignments, followed rules, and left minimal traces behind. His teachers loved him— but didn't *know* him.

One afternoon, a new teacher asked the class to share a project connected to a personal passion. Evan hesitated, then raised his hand. "I built a circuit that powers a tiny wind turbine," he said. The room fell silent—not because it was spectacular, but because no one had imagined this quiet student as inventive or bold.

That day, Evan was seen. And in that moment, his story changed.

This chapter is for every "Evan" who fills our classrooms—the students who are neither struggling nor soaring, whose steady presence keeps the school running smoothly, yet whose potential often waits for someone to notice.

In classrooms filled with noise, movement, and urgency, it is often the quietest students who wait the longest to be noticed. Their needs rarely demand attention, but their growth depends on it. The greatest transformation happens when the quietest student realizes someone finally sees them.

> The greatest transformation happens when the quietest student realizes someone finally sees them.

Framing the Challenge

Every classroom holds a spectrum of need. Educators often focus attention—rightly—on students requiring the most intervention or acceleration. But between the two poles exists a wide band of learners who represent the majority: students who meet benchmarks, behave predictably, and occupy the unlit middle ground.

Recent data highlight the cost of this invisibility. Gallup's 2024 Student Engagement Survey revealed that only thirty-two percent of middle-achieving students described themselves as "highly engaged," a drop of nearly ten points since 2019. Similarly, NAEP trend data (2022) show flat performance among average-scoring students in reading and math while both lower and higher performers demonstrated modest growth. The "excellence gap" widens not just from lack of support but from absence of intentional challenge (Plucker & Puryear, 2023).

Many school improvement plans unintentionally sideline the general education student. Systems prioritize compliance, remediation, or enrichment—but seldom the cultivation of curiosity, belonging, or purpose among those considered "fine." When resources shrink and accountability narrows, the invisible middle fades further from view.

Educational psychologist Carol Dweck reminds us that motivation thrives on feedback, challenge, and recognition (Dweck, 2017). Without those conditions, competence becomes complacency. These students may appear stable, but disengagement grows quietly beneath the surface.

The opportunity before us is not to shift attention *away* from vulnerable populations but to expand the circle of inclusion so that "all means all" truly encompasses every learner. The strategies in this chapter invite educators to reignite purpose, redesign rigor, and re-center belonging for students like Evan—students who deserve to be seen, stretched, and celebrated.

Way 41 — Reignite the Middle: Prioritize Purpose and Curiosity

What?

Middle-of-the-road learners often move through school unnoticed—not because they are disengaged, but because they are compliant. They complete assignments, follow directions, and earn passing grades, yet their learning runs on autopilot. Motivation becomes external: grades, approval, and routine rather than curiosity or meaning. This quiet comfort can mask a deeper disengagement where students stop wondering, questioning, or stretching.

Reigniting the middle requires a shift from performance to purpose. When instruction is designed only to remediate those who are struggling or extend those who excel, the middle is left with work that feels disconnected and uninspiring. Prioritizing purpose and curiosity invites these learners back into learning as thinkers, not just participants.

Why?

Engagement deepens when students understand *why* learning matters. Deci and Ryan's Self-Determination Theory (2023) identifies autonomy and relevance as essential drivers of intrinsic motivation. Yet middle learners rarely experience either. Lessons are often pitched toward catching students up or pushing others ahead, leaving the middle with little voice or challenge.

Over time, this design choice leads to stagnation. Students who are capable but under-stimulated may disengage quietly, contributing just enough to stay invisible. To surface these patterns, **Resource 11.1: Engagement Curve for the Middle Learner** helps educators identify where curiosity declines and compliance replaces authentic engagement.

How?

Reigniting the middle requires intentional design choices that invite curiosity, relevance, and ownership. These steps focus on adult actions that reposition learning as meaningful rather than mechanical.

1. Begin units with purpose mapping

Open each unit by asking, *"Why does this matter beyond school?"* Invite students to brainstorm real-world connections, personal relevance, or future applications. Revisit these ideas at the end of the unit to reflect on how understanding has deepened.

2. Design choice with accountability

Offer tiered options for demonstrating learning—such as podcasts, models, interviews, or visual explanations—while holding expectations for rigor constant. Choice increases autonomy, but accountability ensures depth.

3. Create mini-mentorship opportunities

Pair middle learners with younger peers, community members, or project partners where their learning can make an impact. Teaching or mentoring others often reignites curiosity and confidence in students who feel overlooked.

4. Build structured reflection into routines

Use weekly reflection journals with prompts like, *"Where did curiosity show up for me this week?"* Reflection helps students recognize engagement and signals that curiosity is valued, not incidental.

Reflection Prompts

- When was the last time my middle learners expressed genuine curiosity or wonder?
- Which parts of my instruction prioritize compliance over purpose?
- How often do students have meaningful choices that affect how they learn?
- What signals might suggest quiet disengagement in my classroom?

Then What?

Begin tracking engagement with the same intentionality used for academic growth. Use brief student-voice surveys after each unit to assess whether purpose and curiosity are increasing or stagnating. Analyze results collaboratively to refine design choices and identify patterns across classrooms.

Over time, schools that prioritize purpose see shifts in participation, persistence, and ownership. Middle learners begin to take intellectual risks, ask deeper questions, and re-engage with learning as something done *with* them rather than *to* them.

What If?

What if classrooms measured curiosity alongside test scores? Leaders would design systems that value wonder as much as standards. When schools intentionally reignite the middle, the "forgotten" learner becomes visible again—not through intervention, but through purpose-driven design.

Way 42 — Design for Challenge: Calibrating Rigor for Every Learner

What?

Equity does not mean equal difficulty—it means equal access to stretch. Middle-performing learners are often given work designed to maintain proficiency rather than extend thinking. Tasks are safe, predictable, and rarely demand risk. Over time, this design teaches capable students to aim for completion instead of growth.

Designing for challenge means intentionally calibrating rigor so every learner experiences productive struggle. This requires educators to understand not only what students know, but how they think, feel, and respond when learning becomes demanding. **Resource 11.2: The Invisible Signs of the Middle Learner** supports educators in identifying subtle disengagement and readiness signals that inform when and how to elevate cognitive demand.

Why?

Research consistently confirms that learning accelerates when students are appropriately challenged *and* supported. In his synthesis of over eight hundred meta-analyses, John Hattie identifies teacher expectations (d ≈ 0.43), teacher clarity (d ≈ 0.75), and feedback (d ≈ 0.70) as strong influences on achievement (Hattie, 2021). Together, these influences create the conditions for productive struggle—where students are expected to think deeply, understand success criteria, and receive guidance that moves learning forward.

The issue is not that rigor is ineffective; it is that it is inconsistently applied. Middle learners are often excluded from stretch opportunities because they appear "fine." When challenge is reserved for those already excelling or struggling, capable students remain underdeveloped. Calibrated rigor ensures that challenge is relational—matched to readiness and supported through intentional design rather than withheld out of convenience.

How?

Designing for challenge requires proactive instructional decisions that elevate thinking while preserving access. These steps focus on adult actions that normalize stretch for every learner.

1. Pre-assess to identify readiness for extension

Use brief formative checks to determine which concepts students have already mastered. When proficiency is evident, pivot instruction toward tasks requiring synthesis, transfer, or creative application rather than repetition.

2. Embed cognitive lift into daily tasks

During discussion and collaborative work, intentionally prompt students with higher-order verbs such as *analyze, justify, design, evaluate,* or *innovate.* Cognitive lift signals that deeper thinking is expected—not optional.

3. Use feedback that invites the next layer of thinking

Replace generic praise with feedback that extends learning. Prompts like, *"What's another way to represent this idea?"* or *"How might this apply in a different context?"* reinforce growth over completion.

4. Include middle learners in goal-setting conversations

Use data reflection meetings to help students set personal stretch goals. When average-performing learners are invited into growth discussions, they begin to see challenge as attainable rather than reserved for others.

Reflection Prompts
+ Which students in my classroom consistently meet expectations but are rarely invited to exceed them?
+ How do my tasks encourage struggle rather than repetition?
+ Where might I be unintentionally protecting students from productive challenge?
+ How do clarity and feedback support students when learning becomes demanding?

Then What?
Use formative assessments not to label proficiency, but to locate potential. Share exemplars that model deep thinking and multiple pathways to success. When students see that rigor is supported through guidance and feedback, they become more willing to take intellectual risks.

Over time, classrooms designed for calibrated challenge foster persistence, confidence, and deeper engagement—especially among learners who were previously overlooked.

What If?
What if every lesson plan included a clearly articulated *lift line*—a planned extension designed to elevate thinking for students ready to rise? Leaders would shift conversations from *who needs more support* to *who is ready for deeper challenge*. When rigor is intentionally calibrated, the middle learner is no longer forgotten—they are stretched, seen, and developed.

Way 43 — Strengthen Belonging: Make the Ordinary Student Seen

What?

Belonging is not reserved for students who struggle or stand out—it is a universal need. Yet middle-of-the-road learners often experience conditional belonging. They are welcomed as long as they comply, stay quiet, and do not require attention. Over time, this invisibility teaches students that being "fine" means being unnoticed.

Strengthening belonging means intentionally seeing students not for what they do wrong or exceptionally well, but for who they are. When ordinary students are recognized as individuals—with interests, ideas, and potential—belonging shifts from passive acceptance to active connection.

Why?

Belonging is a powerful predictor of motivation, persistence, and engagement. A 2023 survey by the EdWeek Research Center found that sixty-seven percent of students in the middle performance band reported feeling less connected to their teachers than peers receiving targeted academic or behavioral support. These students are not at immediate risk of failure—but they are at risk of fading.

When students feel unseen, they disengage quietly. Participation narrows, curiosity diminishes, and learning becomes transactional. **Resource 11.3: Student Visibility Map** helps educators analyze which students are consistently seen, heard, and affirmed—and which remain on the margins of school life despite meeting expectations.

How?

Strengthening belonging requires intentional practices that restore visibility without singling students out. These steps focus on adult actions that make connection routine rather than reactive.

1. Practice micro-recognition daily

Develop habits of noticing small but meaningful contributions. A brief comment, a sticky note on a desk, or a short message home acknowledging effort or kindness signals that students are seen beyond performance.

2. Create structured spotlight moments

Once a week, invite one or two students to share an interest, talent, or goal in a low-risk setting. Peers respond with affirmations or reflections, reinforcing that every voice matters.

3. Use advisory time to center growth, not grades

Leverage homeroom or advisory to highlight personal growth, curiosity, and persistence. Belonging grows when students are known for who they are becoming, not just what they produce.

4. Invite students to curate evolving identity maps

Have students create digital or written "About Me" maps that evolve throughout the year. Revisiting these before conferences or recommendations helps teachers respond with intention and care.

Reflection Prompts

- Which students in my classroom are most often described as "fine"?
- How do my routines surface student voice beyond compliance?
- Who receives recognition most often—and who rarely does?
- Where might quiet disengagement be mistaken for contentment?

Then What?

Begin shifting recognition systems to value effort, creativity, collaboration, and kindness—not only high achievement or behavioral compliance. Use visibility data to ensure that every student is intentionally seen across classrooms and settings.

Over time, schools that prioritize belonging for the middle learner see increases in participation, confidence, and persistence. When visibility becomes systemic rather than incidental, engagement rises organically.

What If?

What if schools celebrated steady growth with the same energy given to rapid recovery or acceleration? Leaders would redesign recognition and routines so that being "ordinary" no longer meant being overlooked. When every learner feels seen, achievement follows. Belonging is not a bonus—it is the baseline.

Way 44 — Connect Home and Future: Guiding the Middle Toward Aspiration

What?

Middle-of-the-road learners often move through school meeting expectations without a clear sense of where those efforts lead. They complete requirements, earn credits, and graduate—but rarely connect daily learning to future possibilities. Without intentional guidance, school becomes something to finish rather than something that opens doors.

> Without intentional guidance, school becomes something to finish rather than something that opens doors.

Connecting home and future helps students see learning as a bridge between who they are now and who they are becoming. This work is not about forcing early decisions; it is about expanding horizons, naming transferable skills, and making aspiration visible and attainable. When educators connect present effort to future opportunity, motivation shifts from compliance to purpose.

Why?

Recent data from the National Student Clearinghouse (2024) show that postsecondary enrollment among middle-achieving high school graduates has dropped by nearly six percent since 2019, while enrollment rates for top-performing students have remained above eighty percent. The pattern is clear: students who are neither struggling nor excelling often receive the least guidance, exposure, and mentorship.

This gap is not about ability—it is about access. Middle learners need structured opportunities to explore interests, imagine futures, and see themselves as capable of more than "getting by." When aspiration is left to chance, students without advocacy or clear pathways are most likely to disengage after graduation.

How?

Guiding the middle toward aspiration requires intentional structures that connect learning to life beyond school. These steps focus on adult actions that normalize future-focused conversations for every learner.

1. Embed career curiosity into regular instruction

Integrate brief, monthly career spotlights tied to curriculum themes. For example, a biology unit might feature a local conservationist discussing real-world applications. Short, consistent exposure builds awareness without overwhelm.

2. Hold micro "aspiration conferences"

Use five-minute goal chats to ask three guiding questions: *What do you enjoy learning? What feels challenging but worth the effort? Who do you want to become?* These conversations communicate belief and invite reflection.

3. Expand community partnerships for broad access

Partner with local businesses, organizations, and service agencies to offer micro-internships, shadow days, or project collaborations open to all students—not only those in honors or gifted programs.

4. Develop future-focused portfolios

Have students curate digital portfolios that capture growth, reflections, skills, and accomplishments over time. Portfolios emphasize readiness and progress rather than compliance or grades alone.

To support intentional planning, **Resource 11.4: Purpose-Driven Project Planner** helps educators align instruction, reflection, and future connections so aspiration is built into learning design.

Reflection Prompts

- How often do we connect standards to skills that matter beyond school?
- Which students receive the most exposure to future opportunities—and which receive the least?
- How do our routines invite students to imagine themselves beyond graduation?
- Where might quiet learners need more explicit guidance toward possibility?

Then What?

Begin by auditing who currently receives enrichment, field trips, mentorship, or career exposure opportunities. If those lists mirror gifted or honors rosters, equity remains incomplete. Use audit findings to redesign instructional planning so every student has access to experiences that broaden vision and build confidence.

Over time, schools that intentionally connect home, school, and future see increases in engagement, persistence, and postsecondary participation among middle learners. Aspiration becomes a shared responsibility rather than an individual accident.

What If?

What if every general education student graduated with at least one authentic connection to their future self? Leaders would design systems that guarantee exposure, conversation, and opportunity for all. When aspiration meets access, potential becomes visible—and the middle learner is no longer left wondering what comes next.

Closing Reflection

When Evan's teacher began incorporating curiosity journals, she didn't expect much. He'd always done the work but rarely with spark. One Friday, he wrote: *"I didn't know science could connect to how wind energy powers homes. I might want to study this more."*

Weeks later, the same student who once slipped quietly out of class lingered after dismissal. "Can I borrow some wire for my project?" he asked, eyes bright with intent. The teacher nodded—and recognized something more powerful than completion: *investment.*

The invisible student had been there all along, waiting to be seen not as average, but as capable.

In every school, thousands of Evans cross hallways unnoticed, completing assignments that neither challenge nor inspire. But when educators design with curiosity, belonging, and aspiration in mind, these students step out of the shadows.

Seeing them doesn't mean taking from others—it means widening the lens. When we expand our attention to include those in the middle, we sustain the momentum of *all means all.* Because invisibility is not a lack of ability; it's an absence of attention.

The Constellation of Learning™ Synopsis

The final chapter reflects **Transformational & Adaptive Leadership**, calling attention to "The Invisible Student"—those who quietly meet expectations but rarely receive affirmation. Leadership under this constellation demands that we look beyond visibility metrics to see students who glide beneath the radar.

Transformation begins with recognition. Adaptive leaders create systems that celebrate effort, not just excellence. By designing cultures in which every learner is noticed, nurtured, and needed, we turn invisibility into invitation—and ensure that no student goes unseen again.

By the end of the year, Maya, Avery, and Elena felt safe. They spoke up when something felt wrong. They shared concerns with adults because they trusted someone would listen—and respond.

That trust mattered. As safety and belonging grew, academic growth followed. Literacy improved. Confidence increased. Supports worked better because they were rooted in relationship, not reaction. The system didn't just monitor progress; it adjusted in ways that allowed learning to accelerate.

Their mother, who once called in frustration and fear, became an advocate. She told other families what she experienced—that when concerns were raised, adults listened. That the school didn't get defensive; it got better.

This is what happens when schools choose listening over explaining and partnership over pride. When students trust us, they tell us the truth. When we listen, we learn. And when we act, schools become places where belonging and achievement grow together. Students don't grow because we track them—they grow when they feel safe enough to use their voice.

> Students don't grow because we track them—they grow when they feel safe enough to use their voice.

Hallway Confessions – Daily Practice & Perspective

"I realized I only called on the same six kids," one teacher admitted after a staff reflection session. "They were always quick to answer, and honestly, it kept the pace moving. But when I tracked my interactions, I saw that 60 percent of my class went entire days without a single check-in."

That confession led to a small experiment: the teacher created a "visibility chart," listing each student and marking each meaningful interaction—verbal or nonverbal—daily. Within weeks, patterns shifted. Students who once seemed passive began to participate.

Another teacher added humor: "I started the semester thinking of my quiet students as background music. Now, I realize they're the melody we've been missing."

There's something both humbling and hopeful in that realization. Educators never intend to overlook students; the pace of teaching simply narrows vision. But awareness transforms practice.

Invisibility ends when noticing becomes a habit. Sometimes, it's not about adding new strategies but about changing how we *see*.

The Dismissal Bell – The Five A's

When the final bell rings, our challenge is not to finish the day but to *notice* who leaves unseen. Visibility begins with intention and becomes culture when repeated daily. Every "average" student is a collection of possibilities waiting to be activated. When we notice, stretch, and celebrate them, we transform "fine" into "flourishing."

Action Step	Description
Audit	Who sits quietly in your class, reliable but rarely recognized? Review rosters, participation charts, and classroom interactions. The invisible are often right in front of us.
Adjust	Recalibrate routines. Add moments of choice, challenge, or curiosity. Adjust how you distribute attention—track your interactions for a week and note patterns.
Advocate	Speak their names in data meetings. Share their small victories. Advocate for balance between remediation and enrichment.
Assemble	Collaborate with families and peers. Build small, consistent teams—teachers, EL specialists, counselors, and parents—who meet to celebrate growth and co-design next steps. Sustainable improvement is always a collective act.
Attitude Ask	Will we choose to see the unseen? How will we act then? How will we know when we have reached the unseen? What is different in their persona?

Resources

All resources that are listed throughout the chapters can also be found below. Please utilize them to best support your students.

(Visit www.WhenAllMeansAll.com to access all resources)

Chapter 1

Students in Poverty: Breaking Cycles, Building Pathways to Opportunity

- *Resource 1.1: Barrier Mapping Template* — Monthly chart for identifying and tracking recurring access challenges.
- *Resource 1.2: Belonging Board Guide* — Directions and sample notes for implementing a staff belonging board.
- *Resource 1.3: Barrier Breakers Dashboard Outline* — Dashboard outline tracking attendance, engagement, and support referrals.
- *Resource 1.4: Family Partnership Calendar* — Editable model for planning community-based listening sessions.

Chapter 2

Students with Disabilities: Redefining Ability Through Access and Advocacy

- *Resource 2.1: UDL Checkpoint Planning Guide* — Visual organizer outlining the three UDL principles with reflective questions.
- *Resource 2.2: Co-Teaching Model Selector* — Quick-reference table describing five co-teaching models and use cases.
- *Resource 2.3: Strengths-Based Learner Profile* — Tool for aligning instructional supports around student strengths.
- *Resource 2.4: Data with Dignity Template* — Conversation script for discussing progress using growth-oriented language.
- *Resource 2.5: Belonging Audit Tool* — Checklist reviewing visuals, language, and routines through an inclusion lens.

Chapter 3

Students Experiencing Homelessness: Restoring Stability, Dignity, and Hope

- *Resource 3.1: Student Stability Snapshot* — Snapshot tracking stability, access, and continuity indicators.
- *Resource 3.2: Dignity-Centered Classroom Flexibility Menu* — Menu of dignity-preserving classroom practices without disclosure.
- *Resource 3.3: Continuity of Care Communication Protocol* — Protocol ensuring instructional and relational continuity during transitions.
- *Resource 3.4: Trusted Adult Assignment Tracker* — Leadership tool assigning consistent adult advocates.
- *Resource 3.5: Family Dignity Conversation Guide* — Guide for strength-based, non-compliance family conversations.

Chapter 4

Students from Undocumented Homes: Learning Without Fear, Leading Without Borders

- *Resource 4.1: Sample Family Rights Flyer (Bilingual)* — Bilingual flyer outlining Plyler v. Doe protections.
- *Resource 4.2: Confidentiality Audit Checklist* — Checklist for reviewing enrollment and communication practices.
- *Resource 4.3: Community Partnership Mapping Template* — Template identifying trusted local organizations.
- *Resource 4.4: Safe Zone Poster Template* — Customizable graphic affirming fear-free learning spaces.
- *Resource 4.5: Family Communication Guide* — Examples of trauma-informed inclusive messaging.
- *Resource 4.6: Professional Learning Agenda – Building Trust Beyond the Walls* — 90-minute staff learning agenda with case studies.

Chapter 5

Black Students: Honoring Identity, Driving Equity, and Raising Expectations

- *Resource 5.1: Equity Data Tracker* — Template to disaggregate discipline, grades, and referrals.
- *Resource 5.2: Culturally Responsive Unit Planner* — Backward-design planner embedding identity objectives.
- *Resource 5.3: Dignity-Centered Restorative Framework* — Step-by-step dignity-based conflict resolution framework.
- *Resource 5.4: Joy and Leadership Checklist* — Weekly reflection to spotlight Black student successes.
- *Resource 5.5: Family Engagement Form* — Listening-session questions centered on student strengths.

Chapter 6

Hispanic Students: Culture as Catalyst for Connection

- *Resource 6.1: Cultural Celebration Toolkit* — Activities and recognition strategies for classrooms.
- *Resource 6.2: Parent Newsletter Template* — Bilingual family engagement newsletter template.
- *Resource 6.3: Bilingual Vocabulary Charts* — Cross-language word banks for content areas.
- *Resource 6.4: EL Scaffolding Matrix* — Sample scaffold routines with fading steps.
- *Resource 6.5: Reflection Logs* — Templates for tracking growth, engagement, and identity.

Chapter 7

Native American Students: Restoring Voice, Reviving Tradition, and Reclaiming Space

- *Resource 7.1: Equity & Belonging Checklists* — Checklists examining representation and inclusion.
- *Resource 7.2: Mentorship Program Templates* — Frameworks for culturally grounded mentorship programs.
- *Resource 7.3: Native-Authored Literature & Media List* — Curated list centering Native voices.
- *Resource 7.4: Community Engagement Guide* — Guide for building respectful community partnerships.
- *Resource 7.5: Advisory Council Framework* — Structure for sustained tribal and community voice.

Chapter 8

LGBTQIA+ Students: Belonging Without Exception
- *Resource 8.1: Inclusive Classroom Checklist* — Self-assessment of visuals, language, and practices.
- *Resource 8.2: Cross Content Integration Using LGBTQIA+ Literature* — Text recommendations and cross-content integration guidance.
- *Resource 8.3: SEL Activity Collection* — Activities building resilience and belonging.
- *Resource 8.4: LGBTQIA+ Mental Health Resource Sheet* — Quick-reference national and local support resources.
- *Resource 8.5: Family Engagement Toolkit* — Workshop guides and affirming language for families.
- *Resource 8.6: Peer Mentorship Guide* — Framework for student mentorship and ally programs.

Chapter 9

High-Ability Students: Empowering Potential Beyond the Ceiling
- *Resource 9.1: Depth, Complexity, & Curriculum Compacting Planner* — Planning tool supporting differentiation beyond enrichment.
- *Resource 9.2: High-Ability Learner SEL & Identity Support Guide* — Guide addressing perfectionism, anxiety, and asynchronous development.
- *Resource 9.3: Equitable Gifted Identification & Talent Development Framework* — Framework for equitable identification and talent development.
- *Resource 9.4: Community Mentorship & Passion Project Playbook* — Playbook connecting learners to purpose and community contribution.

Chapter 10

English Learner Students: Language as Bridge, Not Barrier

- *Resource 10.1: EL Proficiency Framework Visual* — Visual distinguishing language proficiency from cognitive ability.
- *Resource 10.2: Instructional Decision Pathway Tool* — Guided tool aligning cognitive demand and language access.
- *Resource 10.3: Rigor Preservation Lens* — Lens for identifying and correcting lowered cognitive demand.
- *Resource 10.4: Scaffold Strategy Menu* — Menu of high-impact scaffolds preserving rigor.

Chapter 11

General Education Students: Illuminating the Invisible Middle

- *Resource 11.1: Engagement Curve for the Middle Learner* — Visual diagnostic distinguishing engagement levels.
- *Resource 11.2: Equity Beyond Intervention Checklist* — Checklist ensuring equity includes middle-performing students.
- *Resource 11.3: Student Visibility Map* — Three-ring model tracking visibility and agency.
- *Resource 11.4: Purpose-Driven Project Planner* — Planner connecting standards to aspiration.

References

Introduction

Balfanz, R., & Byrnes, V. (2023). *The importance of being in school: Chronic absenteeism before and after COVID-19.* Johns Hopkins University Everyone Graduates Center. https://www.attendanceworks.org

Centers for Disease Control and Prevention. (2024). *Youth Risk Behavior Surveillance System (YRBSS): Trends and findings summary, 2023–2024.* U.S. Department of Health and Human Services. https://www.cdc.gov/healthyyouth/data/yrbs

Gallup. (2024). *State of education report 2024.* Gallup, Inc. https://www.gallup.com/education

National Center for Education Statistics. (2024). *The condition of education 2024.* U.S. Department of Education, Institute of Education Sciences. https://nces.ed.gov/programs/coe

National Center for Education Statistics. (2024). English learners in public schools. U.S. Department of Education. https://nces.ed.gov

RAND Corporation. (2024). *Principal turnover: 2024 update on leadership trends and implications for schools.* RAND Education and Labor. https://www.rand.org

TNTP. (2023). *The opportunity myth: 2023 update—What students experience and what educators can do about it.* The New Teacher Project. https://tntp.org

University of Chicago Consortium on School Research. (2020). *Supporting school improvement: Early findings from a reexamination of the 5Essentials survey.* https://consortium.uchicago.edu

Education Week Research Center. (2024). *Teachers, AI, and the classroom: The 2024 survey on emerging technologies in education.* Editorial Projects in Education. https://www.edweek.org

Chapter 1
Students in Poverty: Breaking Cycles, Building Pathways to Opportunity

American Psychological Association. (2023). *Stress and cognitive load among children in financially insecure households.* APA Press.

Attendance Works. (2023). *Reducing chronic absenteeism through community collaboration.* https://www.attendanceworks.org

Cook, C. R., Fiat, A. E., Larson, M., Daikos, C., Slemrod, T., Holland, E. A., & Renshaw, T. L. (2018). *Positive greetings at the door: Evaluation of a low-cost, high-yield proactive classroom management strategy.* Journal of Positive Behavior Interventions, 20(3), 149–159. https://doi.org/10.1177/1098300717753831

Hattie, J., & Zierer, K. (2022). *Visible Learning: The Sequel.* Routledge.

Jeynes, W. (2021). *A meta-analysis on parental involvement and student outcomes.* Urban Education Journal.

National Center for Education Statistics. (2024). *Condition of Education 2024.* U.S. Department of Education.

Rosenthal, R., & Jacobson, L. (2018). *Pygmalion in the Classroom: Teacher Expectation and Pupils' Intellectual Development.* Crown House Publishing.

U.S. Census Bureau. (2023). *Income and poverty in the United States: 2023.* U.S. Department of Commerce.

U.S. Department of Education. (2024). *Student attendance and engagement trends post-pandemic.* Washington, DC.

Chapter 2

Students with Disabilities: Redefining Ability Through Access and Advocacy

CAST. (2022). *Universal Design for Learning Guidelines, version 3.0.* CAST. https://udlguidelines.cast.org

Council for Exceptional Children. (2023). *Special educator shortage report: Trends and implications.* Arlington, VA.

Friend, M., & Cook, L. (2023). *Interactions: Collaboration skills for school professionals* (10th ed.). Pearson.

Gallup. (2023). *Education Index report: Measuring student engagement and belonging.* Gallup, Inc.

National Center on Accessible Educational Materials. (2024). *Meta-analysis of UDL impact on learner engagement.*

National Center on Intensive Intervention. (2024). *Student goal-setting and self-monitoring outcomes.* Washington, DC.

NWEA. (2023). *The state of unfinished learning: Post-pandemic patterns for students with disabilities.* Portland, OR.

Office for Civil Rights. (2023). *Civil rights data collection: Students with disabilities and discipline.* U.S. Department of Education.

U.S. Department of Education. (2024). *The condition of education: Children and youth with disabilities.* Institute of Education Sciences.

Chapter 3

Students Experiencing Homelessness: Restoring Stability, Dignity, and Hope

Institute for Children, Poverty, and Homelessness. (2023). *Annual homeless student report.*

National Center for Homeless Education. (2024). *Federal data summary: School years 2020–2023.* Greensboro, NC: University of North Carolina.

Perry, B. D., & Winfrey, O. (2021). *What happened to you? Conversations on trauma, resilience, and healing.* Flatiron Books.

SAMHSA. (2022). *Trauma and youth resilience in schools.* Washington, DC: U.S. Department of Health and Human Services.

Search Institute. (2023). *Relationships that matter: Mentoring and belonging among youth in transition.* Minneapolis, MN.

Chapter 4
Students from Undocumented Homes: Learning Without Fear, Leading Without Borders

American Psychological Association. (2022). *Immigrant family stress and student mental health: Implications for schools.* APA Publishing.

Gándara, P., & Ee, J. (2021). *The impact of immigration enforcement on the nation's schools.* Civil Rights Project, UCLA.

Migration Policy Institute. (2023). *K–12 education and immigrant families in the United States.* Washington, DC: Author.

National Center for Community Schools. (2024). *Community partnerships and student outcomes report.* New York, NY: Children's Aid.

National Immigration Law Center. (2023). *Immigrant access to education: Rights and realities.* NILC Publications.

Pew Research Center. (2023). *Facts on immigrants and U.S. immigration policies.* Pew Research Center.

Suárez-Orozco, C., Yoshikawa, H., & Tseng, V. (2023). *Learning in the shadows: Immigrant students and school belonging.* Harvard Education Press.

U.S. Department of Education. (2023). *Fact sheet: Information on the rights of all children to enroll in public schools.* Washington, DC: Author.

Chapter 5
Black Students: Honoring Identity, Driving Equity, and Raising Expectations

EdTrust. (2023). *Equity in curriculum and representation: A national audit.* Education Trust.

Gregory, A., Skiba, R., & Noguera, P. (2022). *Eliminating disparities in school discipline: A framework for intervention. Review of Educational Research, 92*(1), 56-89.

Hammond, Z. (2020). *Culturally responsive teaching and the brain* (2nd ed.). Corwin.

Ladson-Billings, G. (2021). *Culturally relevant pedagogy: Asking a different question (25th anniversary ed.).* Teachers College Press.

Nasir, N., & Snyder, C. (2022). Positive racial identity and student outcomes: The role of joy in learning. *Journal of Black Education Research,* 18(2), 85-104.

Oakland Unified School District. (2023). *Equity report on restorative practices outcomes 2018–2023.*

Obama Foundation. (2023). *My Brother's Keeper Alliance impact report.*

Rosenthal, R., & Jacobson, L. (1968/2022). *Pygmalion in the classroom: Teacher expectation and pupils' intellectual development (Updated ed.).* Crown.

U.S. Department of Education, Office for Civil Rights. (2023). *Civil Rights Data Collection: School climate and safety.*

University of Chicago Consortium on School Research. (2023). *Building trust and reducing discipline disparities: Findings from CPS equity initiatives.*

Chapter 6

Hispanic Students: Culture as Catalyst for Connection

August, D., & Shanahan, T. (2023). *Developing literacy in second-language learners: Report of the National Literacy Panel on Language-Minority Children and Youth.* Routledge.

Gay, G. (2018). *Culturally responsive teaching: Theory, research, and practice* (3rd ed.). Teachers College Press.

National Center for Education Statistics (NCES). (2023). *The Condition of Education 2023.* U.S. Department of Education.

U.S. Department of Education. (2022). *Graduation rates by student demographics.* https://www.ed.gov

Chapter 7

Native American Students: Restoring Voice, Reviving Tradition, and Reclaiming Space

Brave Heart, M. Y. H. (2022). *Historical trauma and Native American youth well-being.* Journal of Indigenous Studies, 15(2), 45–62.

Brayboy, B. M. J., & Maughan, E. (2023). *Culturally responsive schooling for Native American students.* Educational Research Review, 30, 100–115.

Gay, G. (2022). *Culturally responsive teaching: Theory, research, and practice* (3rd ed.). Teachers College Press.

Lomawaima, K., & McCarty, T. (2023). *To remain an Indian: Lessons in education and sovereignty.* Harvard University Press.

NCES. (2023). *Public school student enrollment by race/ethnicity.* U.S. Department of Education.

National Indian Education Study. (2022). *Findings on student engagement and cultural inclusion.* NCES.

Pierce, M. (2022). *Identity, culture, and academic achievement in Indigenous classrooms.* Journal of Educational Equity, 12(3), 58–74.

U.S. Department of Education. (2023). *Graduation rates by student group.* https://www.ed.gov/data

Chapter 8

LGBTQIA+ Students: Belonging Without Exception

CASEL. (2022). *What is SEL?* Collaborative for Academic, Social, and Emotional Learning. https://casel.org/what-is-sel

Family Acceptance Project. (2022). *Family acceptance of LGBTQ youth protects against depression, substance abuse, and suicide.* San Francisco State University.Human Rights Campaign Foundation. (2023). *2023 LGBTQ+ youth report.*

https://reports.hrc.org/2023-lgbtq-youth-report

GLSEN. (2022). *2022 National School Climate Survey: The experiences of LGBTQ+ youth in our nation's schools.* https://www.glsen.org/research/2022-national-school-climate-survey

The Trevor Project. (2023). *2023 U.S. national survey on the mental health of LGBTQ young people.*
https://www.thetrevorproject.org/survey-2023/

Chapter 9
High-Ability Students: Empowering Potential Beyond the Ceiling

Card, D., & Giuliano, L. (2023). *Universal screening increases the representation of underrepresented minorities in gifted education. American Economic Journal: Applied Economics, 15*(2), 195–227.

Missett, T. C., Azano, A. P., & Rinn, A. N. (2023). *Equity and excellence in gifted education: Advancing culturally responsive identification and service. Gifted Child Quarterly, 67*(1), 5–20.

National Association for Gifted Children. (2024). *State of the states in gifted education: 2022–2023 report.* Washington, DC: Author.

Neihart, M., & Betts, G. T. (2023). *Profiles of the gifted and talented (revised). Roeper Review, 45*(3), 200–212.

Reis, S. M., & Renzulli, J. S. (2022). *Enrichment and differentiation for all learners: Revisiting the schoolwide enrichment model. Educational Leadership, 79*(8), 20–25.

U.S. Department of Education, National Center for Education Statistics. (2023). *Digest of Education Statistics: 2023.* Washington, DC: Author.

Chapter 10
English Learner Students: Language as Bridge, Not Barrier

Echevarría, J., Vogt, M., & Short, D. J. (2017). *Making Content Comprehensible for English Learners: The SIOP Model* (5th ed.). Pearson.

García, O., & Kleifgen, J. A. (2022). *Educating Emergent Bilinguals: Policies, Programs, and Practices for English Learners* (3rd ed.). Teachers College Press.

Henderson, A. T., Mapp, K. L., & Johnson, V. R. (2022). *Beyond the Bake Sale: The Essential Guide to Family–School Partnerships* (2nd ed.). The New Press.

Honigsfeld, A., & Dove, M. G. (2022). *Co-Teaching for English Learners: Driving Instructional Excellence* (2nd ed.). Corwin Press.

National Academies of Sciences, Engineering, and Medicine. (2023). *Promoting the Educational Success of English Learners: Current Challenges and Future Directions.* The National Academies Press.

Office of English Language Acquisition (OELA). (2024). *Advancing Multilingual Education: National Data Brief.* U.S. Department of Education.

Office of English Language Acquisition (OELA). (2024). *National Data Brief: Integrated Instructional Models for Multilingual Learners.* U.S. Department of Education.

Paris, D., & Alim, H. S. (2022). *Culturally Sustaining Pedagogies: Teaching and Learning for Justice in a Changing World* (2nd ed.). Teachers College Press.

Sugarman, J., & Geary, C. (2023). *Advancing Multilingual Education in U.S. Schools.* Migration Policy Institute.

U.S. Department of Education, Office of English Language Acquisition. (2023). *Profiles of English Learners in U.S. Public Schools, 2022 Update.*

Zwiers, J. (2020). *Academic Language Mastery: Conversational Discourse in Context.* Corwin Press.

Chapter 11

General Education Students: Illuminating the Invisible Middle

Deci, E. L., & Ryan, R. M. (2023). *Self-determination theory in schools: Autonomy, engagement, and well-being.* Educational Psychologist, 58(4), 233–249.

Dweck, C. S. (2017). *Mindset: The new psychology of success.* Random House.

Gallup. (2024). *Student Engagement Survey Results 2024.* Gallup Education.

Hattie, J. (2021). *Visible learning: The sequel.* Routledge.

Plucker, J. A., & Puryear, J. S. (2023). *The excellence gap revisited: A decade of progress?* Journal for the Education of the Gifted, 46(2), 127–149.

Acknowledgements

This book is the result of a collective effort shaped by countless conversations, courageous questions, and shared commitments to students. While our names appear on the cover, this work exists because of the people and communities who challenged us to think deeper, lead better, and act with greater urgency on behalf of children.

We are deeply grateful to the educators, leaders, and support staff across schools and districts who invited us into their classrooms, buildings, and systems. Your honesty about what is working—and what is not—kept this work grounded in reality. You trusted us with your stories, your struggles, and your hopes for students, and we carry that responsibility seriously.

We owe particular thanks to the colleagues and collaborators who pushed our thinking and sharpened our practice. Through coaching sessions, keynotes, planning meetings, and late-night debriefs, you helped refine the ideas that live in these pages. Your willingness to wrestle with hard truths and resist surface-level solutions strengthened both this book and our belief that meaningful change is possible.

To our mentors—those who modeled courage, clarity, and conviction—we are thankful for the standards you set and the questions you refused to let us avoid. You reminded us that leadership is not about comfort or compliance, but about responsibility and moral purpose.

Special thanks to Jimmy Casas for his belief in our vision and giving us the space, creativity, and pathway to make this a reality. We also appreciate our editor Jeff Zoul and the rest of the team at ConnectEdd, for the talent, support, and service provided in the final motions from editing to publication to implementation.

Kate Gagnon was Adam's first editor for *Instructional Change Agent*. Kate's advice, feedback, and organization influenced the way in which we structured the development of this book. Your skillset continues to make a difference,

Finally, we extend our deepest appreciation to our families for their patience, encouragement, and unwavering belief in this work. You made space for long hours, deep reflection, and the emotional weight that comes with writing about students we care so deeply about. Your support made this book possible.

This work belongs with all of you, too.

About the Authors

D r. **Adam Drummond-Konopasek** is an award-winning educational leader, author, and national keynote speaker committed to ensuring each student is seen, supported, and positioned to thrive. A former principal recognized as Indiana Northeast Principal of the Year, Adam has led schools and districts through meaningful, student-centered change grounded in both research and real-world practice. He currently serves as a Senior Director, author, and keynoter with Center for Model Schools, partnering with educators nationwide to strengthen leadership, culture, and instructional impact—especially for students who have been historically marginalized or overlooked.

Danny **Drummond-Konopasek** is a veteran educator, leadership and instructional coach, and national speaker dedicated to building schools where students feel safe, valued, and empowered to learn. His experience includes middle and high school teaching in both private and public schools, as well as coordinating within the student services division of Wisconsin's fifth-largest school district. Through his coaching work, Danny brings deep expertise in social-emotional learning, trauma-informed practices, and systems that translate compassion into consistent, school-wide action that improves outcomes for all learners.

Together, Adam and Danny are co-owners of DK Education Collaborative, partnering with schools and districts to identify student groups too often left behind and align leadership and instructional actions that redirect school trajectories, improve student outcomes, and restore hope for each student and educator.

More from ConnectEDD Publishing

Since 2015, ConnectEDD has worked to transform education by empowering educators to become better-equipped to teach, learn, and lead. What started as a small company designed to provide professional learning events for educators has grown to include a variety of services to help educators and administrators address essential challenges. ConnectEDD offers instructional and leadership coaching, professional development workshops focusing on a variety of educational topics, a roster of nationally recognized educator associates who possess hands-on knowledge and experience, educational conferences custom-designed to meet the specific needs of schools, districts, and state/national organizations, and ongoing, personalized support, both virtually and onsite. In 2020, ConnectEDD expanded to include publishing services designed to provide busy educators with books and resources consisting of practical information on a wide variety of teaching, learning, and leadership topics. Please visit us online at connecteddpublishing.com or contact us at: info@connecteddpublishing.com

Recent Publications:

Live Your Excellence: Action Guide by Jimmy Casas

Culturize: Action Guide by Jimmy Casas

Daily Inspiration for Educators: Positive Thoughts for Every Day of the Year by Jimmy Casas

Eyes on Culture: Multiply Excellence in Your School by Emily Paschall

Pause. Breathe. Flourish. Living Your Best Life as an Educator by William D. Parker

L.E.A.R.N.E.R. Finding the True, Good, and Beautiful in Education by Marita Diffenbaugh

Educator Reflection Tips Volume II: Refining Our Practice by Jami Fowler-White

Handle With Care: Managing Difficult Situations in Schools with Dignity and Respect by Jimmy Casas and Joy Kelly

Disruptive Thinking: Preparing Learners for Their Future by Eric Sheninger

Permission to be Great: Increasing Engagement in Your School by Dan Butler

Daily Inspiration for Educators: Positive Thoughts for Every Day of the Year, Volume II by Jimmy Casas

The 6 Literacy Levers: Creating a Community of Readers by Brad Gustafson

The Educator's ATLAS: Your Roadmap to Engagement by Weston Kieschnick

In This Season: Words for the Heart by Todd Nesloney, LaNesha Tabb, Tanner Olson, and Alice Lee

Leading with a Humble Heart: A 40-Day Devotional for Leaders by Zac Bauermaster

Recalibrate the Culture: Our Why…Our Work…Our Values by Jimmy Casas

Creating Curious Classrooms: The Beauty of Questions by Emma Chiappetta

Crafting the Culture: 45 Reflections on What Matters Most by Joe Sanfelippo and Jeffrey Zoul

Improving School Mental Health: The Thriving School Community Solution by Charle Peck and Dr. Cameron Caswell

Building Authenticity: A Blueprint for the Leader Inside You by Todd Nesloney and Tyler Cook

Connecting Through Conversation: A Playbook for Talking with Kids by Erika Bare and Tiffany Burns

The Dream Factory: Designing a Purposeful Life by Mark Trumbo

Stories Behind Stances: Creating Empathy Through Hearing "The Other Side" by Chris Singleton

Happy Eyes: Becoming All Things to All People by Ryan Tillman

The Generative Age: Artificial Intelligence and the Future of Education by Alana Winnick

Recalibrate the Culture: Action Guide by Jimmy Casas

Leading with PEOPLE: A Six Pillar Framework for Fruitful Leadership by Zac Bauermaster

A School Leader's Guide to Reclaiming Purpose by Frederick C. Buskey

Foundations of an Elite Culture: Building Success with High Standards and a Positive Environment by David Arencibia

Personalize: Meeting the Needs of All Learners by Eric Sheninger and Nicki Slaugh

The Five Principles of Educator Professionalism: Rebuilding Trust in Schools by Nason Lollar

Words on the Wall: Culturizing Your Classroom For Observable Impact by Jimmy Casas and Cale Birk

School of Engagement: 45 Activities to Ignite Student Learning by Jonathan Alsheimer

Intentional Instructional Moves: Strategic Steps to Accelerate Student Learning by Sherry St. Clair

Overcoming Education: Complex Challenges, Difficult People, and the Art of Making a Difference by Brad R. Gustafson

The Language of Behavior: A Framework to Elevate Student Success by Charle Peck and Joshua Stamper

Whose Permission Are You Waiting For? An Educator's Guide to Doing What You Love by William D. Parker

The Leader You're Not…And Why It's Just As Important As the Leader You Are by Scott Borba

The Growth-Minded Leader by Tyler Cook

Day by Day: 180 Days of Hope and Encouragement by Zac Bauermaster

Make Your Move: For Ambitious People Ready to Live Their Aspirations by Marlon Styles, Jr.

The Hidden Work: What Separates Top Performers From Underachievers by Weston Kieschnick

Lifted to Lead: How a Paraplegic Orphan Rose from the Streets of Saigon to Become an American Leader by Stefan Bean and Kathy Nash

Lead From Who You Are: The Personal, People, and Process Rhythms of Meaningful Leadership by Joe Sanfelippo

Ready to Lead with AI: A Practical Guide for School Leaders by Kip Glazer

www.ingramcontent.com/pod-product-compliance
Lightning Source LLC
Chambersburg PA
CBHW071455140726
47997CB00005B/1739